Table of Contents

Helen of Troy

Annotated

Andrew Lang

Categorie(s): Fiction, Poetry, Fairy Tales, Folk Tales & Mythology

About Lang:

Andrew Lang (March 31, 1844, Selkirk – July 20, 1912, Banchory, Kincardineshire) was a prolific Scots man of letters. He was a poet, novelist, and literary critic, and contributor to anthropology. He now is best known as the collector of folk and fairy tales. The Andrew Lang lectures at St Andrews University are named for him.

"Le joyeulx temps passé souloit estre occasion que je faisoie de plaisants diz et gracieuses chançonnetes et ballades. Mais je me suis mis à faire cette traittié d'affliction contre ma droite nature … et suis content de l'avoir prinse, car mes douleurs me semblent en estre allegées."—*Le Romant de Troilus.*

To all old Friends; to all who dwell
Where Avon dhu and Avon gel
Down to the western waters flow
Through valleys dear from long ago;
To all who hear the whisper'd spell
Of Ken; and Tweed like music swell
Hard by the Land Debatable,
Or gleaming Shannon seaward go,—
To all old Friends!

To all that yet remember well
What secrets Isis had to tell,
How lazy Cherwell loiter'd slow
Sweet aisles of blossom'd May below—
Whate'er befall, whate'er befell,
To *all* old Friends.

Part 1
THE COMING OF PARIS

Of the coming of Paris to the house of Menelaus, King of
Lacedaemon, and of the tale Paris told concerning his past life.

I.

All day within the palace of the King
In Lacedaemon, was there revelry,
Since Menelaus with the dawn did spring
Forth from his carven couch, and, climbing high
The tower of outlook, gazed along the dry
White road that runs to Pylos through the plain,
And mark'd thin clouds of dust against the sky,
And gleaming bronze, and robes of purple stain.

II.

Then, at that point cried he to his serving men, what not

Obey'd him, and their work didn't extra,

Furthermore, ladies set out tables through the corridor,

Light polish'd tables, with the material reasonable.

Also, water from the all around did others bear,

Also, the great house-spouse hectically delivered

Meats from her store, and stinted not the uncommon

Wine from Ismarian grape plantations of the North.

III.

The men drave up a yearling from the field

For penance, and sheath'd her horns with gold;

Also, solid Boethous the hatchet used

Also, destroyed her; on the productive earth she roll'd,

Also, they her appendages partitioned; overlap on overlay

They laid the fat, and cast upon the fire

The grain. Such ceremonies were fashioned of old

At the point when everything was order'd as the Gods want.

IV.

Furthermore, presently the chariots came underneath the trees

Hard by the royal residence gateways, in the shade,

Furthermore, Menelaus knew King Diocles

Of Pherae, sprung of a despondent servant

Whom the incomparable Elian River God betray'd

In the still watches of a mid year night,

When by his dark green water-course she stray'd

Also, lean'd to cull his water-lilies white.

V.

Other than King Diocles there sat a man

Of all men mortal sure the most attractive far,

For o'er his purple robe Sidonian

His yellow hair sparkled more splendid than the star

Of the long brilliant locks that bodeth war;

His face resembled the daylight, and his blue

Happy eyes no distress had the spell to deface

Were clear as skies the tempest hath thunder'd through.

VI.

Then, at that point Menelaus spake unto his society,

Furthermore, anxious at his promise they ran amain,

Furthermore, loosed the perspiring ponies from the burden,

Furthermore, cast before them spelt, and grain.

Also, lean'd the polish'd vehicle, with brilliant rein,

Against the sparkling spaces of the divider;

Also, called the ocean wanderers who follow'd fain

Inside the pillar'd front courts of the corridor.

VII.

The more peculiar sovereign was follow'd by a band

Of men, all clad like meanderers of the ocean,

What's more, brown'd were they just like the desert sand,

Uproarious in their jollity, and of their bearing free;

Furthermore, gifts they bore, from the profound depository

Furthermore, timberlands of some far away Eastern master,

Jars of gold, and bronze, and ivory,

That may the Pythian fane have over-put away.

VIII.

Presently when the King had welcomed Diocles

Also, him that seem'd his visitor, the twain were driven

To the faint polish'd showers, where, for their simplicity,

Cool water o'er their brilliant appendages was shed;

With oil blessed was each goodly head

By Asteris and Phylo reasonable of face;

Then, similar to two divine beings for beauty, they sped

To Menelaus in the meal place.

IX.

There were they situated at the King's right hand,

What's more, ladies exposed them bread, and meat, and wine,

Inside that reasonable lobby of the Argive land

Whose entryways and rooftop with gold and silver sparkle

As doth the home of Zeus divine.

Also, Helen came from forward her fragrant nook

The most attractive woman of eternal line,

Like morning, when the ruddy sunrise doth bloom.

X.

Adraste set for her a sparkling seat,

Well-created of cedar-wood and ivory;

Also, delightful Alcippe drove the reasonable,

The well-cherished kid, Hermione,—

Somewhat lady of long summers three—

Her star-like head on Helen's bosom she laid,

What's more, peep'd out at the outsiders contemplatively

Just like the wont of kids half apprehensive.

XI.

Presently when want of meat and drink was finished,

What's more, finished was the delight of minstrelsy,

Sovereign Helen spake, seeing how the sun

Inside the paradise of bronze was enjoying some real success:

"Really, my companions, methinks the hour is near

At the point when men might ache for to realize what require
doth bring

To Lacedaemon, o'er wet ways and dry,

This sovereign that bears the staff of a ruler?

XII.

"Yea, or perchance a God is he, for still

The incomparable Gods meander on our human ways,

What's more, watch their special stepped areas upon mead or
slope

What's more, taste our penance, and hear our lays,

What's more, presently, perchance, will regard if any implores,

Also, presently will vex us with harsh control,

Be that as it may, anywise should man experience his days,

For Fate hath given him a suffering soul.

XIII.

"Then, at that point advise us, prithee, all that might be told,

Furthermore, if thou workmanship a human, happiness be thine!

Also, on the off chance that thou workmanship a God, rich with gold

Thine raised area in our castle court will sparkle,

With roses garlanded and wet with wine,

Also, we will laud you with persistent breath;

Ok, then, at that point be delicate as thou craftsmanship divine,

Also, bring not on us evil Love or Death!"

XIV.

Then, at that point spake the outsider,— as when to a house cleaner

A young fellow talks, his voice was delicate and low,—

"Oh, no God am I; be not apprehensive,

For even presently the gesturing daisies develop

Whose seed over my verdant cairn will blow,

At the point when I am only a float of white

Residue in a cruse of gold; and nothing know

Be that as it may, dimness, and incomprehensible Night.

XV.

"The sunrise, or early afternoon, or dusk, draweth close

At the point when one will destroy me on the extension of war,

Or then again with the heartless blade, or with the lance,

Or then again with the harsh bolt flying far.

In any case, as a man's heart, so his great days are,

That Zeus, the Lord of Thunder, giveth him,

Wherefore I follow Fortune, similar to a star,

Whate'er might stand by me somewhere far off faint.

XVI.

"Presently all men call me Paris, Priam's child,

Who broadly controls a tranquil people and still.

Nay, however ye abide a far distance off, there is none

Yet, knows about Ilios on the breezy slope,

What's more, of the plain that the two waterways fill

With mumbling sweet streams the entire extended,

Furthermore, dividers the Gods have created with wondrous ability

Where cometh never man to treat us terribly.XVII.

"Wherefore I sail'd not here for help in war,
Though well the Argives in such need can aid.
The force that comes on me is other far;
One that on all men comes: I seek the maid
Whom golden Aphrodite shall persuade
To lay her hand in mine, and follow me,
To my white halls within the cedar shade
Beyond the waters of the barren sea."

XVIII.

Then at the Goddess' name grew Helen pale,
Like golden stars that flicker in the dawn,
Or like a child that hears a dreadful tale,
Or like the roses on a rich man's lawn,
When now the suns of Summer are withdrawn,
And the loose leaves with a sad wind are stirr'd,
Till the wet grass is strewn with petals wan,—
So paled the golden Helen at his word.

XIX.

But swift the rose into her cheek return'd
And for a little moment, like a flame,
The perfect face of Argive Helen burn'd,
As doth a woman's, when some spoken name
Brings back to mind some ancient love or shame,
But none save Paris mark'd the thing, who said,
"My tale no more must weary this fair dame,
With telling why I wander all unwed."

XX.

But Helen, bending on him gracious brows,
Besought him for the story of his quest,
"For sultry is the summer, that allows
To mortal men no sweeter boon than rest;
And surely such a tale as thine is best
To make the dainty-footed hours go by,
Till sinks the sun in darkness and the West,
And soft stars lead the Night along the sky."

XXI.

Then at the word of Helen Paris spoke,
"My tale is shorter than a summer day,—
My mother, ere I saw the light, awoke,
At dawn, in Ilios, shrieking in dismay,
Who dream'd that 'twixt her feet there fell and lay
A flaming brand, that utterly burn'd down
To dust of crumbling ashes red and grey,
The coronal of towers and all Troy town.

XXII.

"Then the interpretation of this dream
My father sought at many priestly hands,
Where the white temple doth in Pytho gleam,
And at the fane of Ammon in the sands,
And where the oak tree of Dodona stands
With boughs oracular against the sky,—
And with one voice the Gods from all the lands,
Cried out, 'The child must die, the child must die.'

XXIII.

"Then was I born to sorrow; and in fear
The dark priest took me from my sire, and bore
A wailing child through beech and pinewood drear,
Up to the knees of Ida, and the hoar
Rocks whence a fountain breaketh evermore,
And leaps with shining waters to the sea,
Through black and rock-wall'd pools without a shore,—
And there they deem'd they took farewell of me.

XXIV.

"But round my neck they tied a golden ring
That fell from Ganymedes when he soar'd
High over Ida on the eagle's wing,
To dwell for ever with the Gods adored,
To be the cup-bearer beside the board
Of Zeus, and kneel at the eternal throne,—
A jewel 'twas from old King Tros's hoard,
That ruled in Ilios ages long agone.

XXV.

"And there they left me in that dell untrod,—
Shepherd nor huntsman ever wanders there,
For dread of Pan, that is a jealous God,—
Yea, and the ladies of the streams forbear
The Naiad nymphs, to weave their dances fair,
Or twine their yellow tresses with the shy
Fronds of forget-me-not and maiden-hair,—
There had the priests appointed me to die.

XXVI.

"But vainly doth a man contend with Fate!
My father had less pity on his son
Than wild things of the woodland desolate.
'Tis said that ere the Autumn day was done
A great she-bear, that in these rocks did wonn,
Beheld a sleeping babe she did convey
Down to a den beheld not of the sun,
The cavern where her own soft litter lay.

XXVII.

"And therein was I nurtured wondrously,
So Rumour saith: I know not of these things,
For mortal men are ever wont to lie,
Whene'er they speak of sceptre-bearing kings:
I tell what I was told, for memory brings
No record of those days, that are as deep
Lost as the lullaby a mother sings
In ears of children that are fallen on sleep.

XXVIII.

"Men say that now five autumn days had pass'd,
When Agelaus, following a hurt deer,
Trod soft on crackling acorns, and the mast
That lay beneath the oak and beech-wood sere,
In dread lest angry Pan were sleeping near,
Then heard a cry from forth a cavern grey,
And peeping round the fallen rocks in fear,
Beheld where in the wild beast's tracks I lay.

XXIX.

"So Agelaus bore me from the wild,
Down to his hut; and with his children I
Was nurtured, being, as was deem'd, the child
Of Hermes, or some mountain deity;
For these with the wild nymphs are wont to lie
Within the holy caverns, where the bee
Can scarcely find a darkling path to fly
Through veils of bracken and the ivy-tree.

XXX.

"So with the shepherds on the hills I stray'd,
And drave the kine to feed where rivers run,
And play'd upon the reed-pipe in the shade,
And scarcely knew my manhood was begun,
The pleasant years still passing one by one,
Till I was chiefest of the mountain men,
And clomb the peaks that take the snow and sun,
And braved the anger'd lion in his den.

XXXI.

"Now in my herd of kine was one more dear
By far than all the rest, and fairer far;
A milkwhite bull, the captive of my spear,
And all the wondering shepherds called him *Star*:
And still he led his fellows to the war,
When the lean wolves against the herds came down,
Then would he charge, and drive their hosts afar
Beyond the pastures to the forests brown.

XXXII.

"Now so it chanced that on an autumn morn,
King Priam sought a goodly bull to slay
In memory of his child, no sooner born
Than midst the lonely mountains cast away,
To die ere scarce he had beheld the day;
And Priam's men came wandering afar
To that green pool where by the flocks I lay,
And straight they coveted the goodly *Star*,

XXXIII.

"And drave him, no word spoken, to the town:
One man mine arrow lit on, and he fell;
His comrades held me off, and down and down,
Through golden windings of the autumn dell,
They spurr'd along the beast that loved me well,
Till red were his white sides; I following,
Wrath in my heart, their evil deeds to tell
In Ilios, at the footstool of the King.

XXXIV.

"But ere they came to the God-builded wall,
They spied a meadow by the water-side,
And there the men of Troy were gathered all
For joust and play; and Priam's sons defied
All other men in all Maeonia wide
To strive with them in boxing and in speed.
Victorious with the shepherds had I vied,
So boldly followed to that flowery mead.

XXXV.

"Maeonia, Phrygia, Troia there were met,
And there the King, child of Laomedon,
Rich prizes for the vanquishers had set,
Damsels, and robes, and cups that like the sun
Shone, but the white bull was the chiefest one;
And him the victor in the games should slay
To Zeus, the King of Gods, when all was done,
And so with sacrifice should crown the day.

XXXVI.

"Now it were over long, methinks, to tell
The contest of the heady charioteers,
Of them the goal that turn'd, and them that fell.
But I outran the young men of my years,
And with the bow did I out-do my peers,
And wrestling; and in boxing, over-bold,
I strove with Hector of the ashen spears,
Yea, till the deep-voiced Heralds bade us hold.

XXXVII.

"Then Priam hail'd me winner of the day;
Mine were the maid, the cup, and chiefest prize,
Mine own fair milkwhite bull was mine to slay;
But then the murmurs wax'd to angry cries,
And hard men set on me in deadly wise,
My brethren, though they knew it not; I turn'd,
And fled unto the place of sacrifice,
Where altars to the God of strangers burn'd.

XXXVIII.

"At mine own funeral feast, had I been slain,
But, fearing Zeus, they halted for a space,
And lo, Apollo's priestess with a train
Of holy maidens came into that place,
And far did she outshine the rest in grace,
But in her eyes such dread was frozen then
As glares eternal from the Gorgon's face
Wherewith Athene quells the ranks of men.

XXXIX.

"She was old Priam's girl, some time in the past

Apollo adored her, and didn't deny

His gifts,— the things that are to be to know,

The tongue of sooth-saying that can't lie,

Furthermore, information gave he of all birds that fly

'Neath paradise; but then his supplication did she scorn.

So he his gifts jumbled totally,

What's more, sooth she saith, yet evermore to no end.

XL.

"She, when her dim eyes fell on me, stood

At look some time, with wan lips mumbling,

And afterward came near to me, and grasped my hand,

What's more, driven me to the hassock of the King,

What's more, call'd me 'sibling,' and drew forward the ring

That men had found upon me in nature,

For still I bore it as something valuable,

The badge of a dad to his youngster.

XLI.

"This sign Cassandra show'd to Priam: straight

The King wax'd pale, and ask'd what this may be?

Also, she made answer, 'Sir, and King, thy destiny

That goes to all men conceived hath come on you;

This shepherd is thine own youngster verily:

How prefer to thine his shape, his temple, his hands!

Nay there is none however hath the eyes to see

That here the youngster tragically missing to Troia stands.'

XLII.

"Then, at that point the King uncovered me to his elevated corridor,

Also, there we ate in much love and merriment,

Also, Priam to the mountain sent for all

That knew me, and the way of my introduction to the world:

Also, presently among the extraordinary ones of the earth

In regal robe and state see me set,

Also, something fell I dread not; even shortage,

Whate'er the Gods recall or neglect.

XLIII.

"My new rich life had grown something typical,

The lovely years actually passing individually,

At the point when somewhere down in Ida was I meandering

The glare of very much assembled Ilios to evade,

In summer, ere the day was completely done,

At the point when I viewed a goodly ruler,— the hair

To sprout upon his lip had scant started,—

The season when the bloom of youth is reasonable.

XLIV.

"Then, at that point knew I Hermes by his brilliant wand

Wherewith he quiets the eyes of men to rest;

However, gesturing with his foreheads, he bade me stand,

Also, spake, 'To-night thou hast a tryst to keep,

With Goddesses inside the woods profound;

Also, Paris, stunning things shalt thou see,

More reasonable than they for what men war and sob,

Realms, and distinction, and triumphs, and gold.

XLV.

"'For, lo! to-night inside the timberland faint

Do Aphrodite and Athene meet,

Also, Hera, who to you will uncovered every appendage,

Each effortlessness from brilliant head to ivory feet,

Furthermore, you, reasonable shepherd Paris, they implore

As thou 'mongst men workmanship beauteous, to pronounce

Which Queen of Queens interminable is generally sweet,

Furthermore, doth merit the meed of the most reasonable.

XLVI.

"'For late between them rose an unpleasant hardship

In Peleus' lobbies upon his big day,

At the point when Peleus took him an undying spouse,

Furthermore, there was bidden all the God's exhibit,

Save Discord just; yet she brought alarm,

Also, cast an apple on the wedding board,

With "Let the most attractive bear the prize away"

Profound on its brilliant skin and shining scored.

XLVII.

"'Presently in the unexpected evening, whenas the sun

In Tethys' silver arms hath rested 60 minutes,

Shalt thou be had into the backwoods dun,

Furthermore, brought unto a dull charmed arbor,

Also, there of Goddesses see the bloom

With very magnificence consuming in the evening,

Also, these will offer Wisdom, Love, and Power;

Then, at that point, Paris, be thou savvy, and pick aright!'

XLVIII.

"He spake, and pass'd, and Night without a breath,

Without a star drew on; and presently I heard

The voice that in the springtime wandereth,

The crying of Dame Hera's shadowy bird;

Furthermore, soon the quiet of the trees was blended

By the insightful fowl of Pallas; and anigh,

More sweet than is a young lady's initially adoring word,

The pigeons of Aphrodite made answer.

XLIX.

"These voices did I finish the trees,

Stringing the coppice 'neath a black sky,

When, lo! the actual Queen of Goddesses,

In brilliant excellence sparkling wondrously,

Indeed, even she that hath the Heaven for covering,

Furthermore, in the arms of strong Zeus doth rest,—

And afterward for fear methought that I should kick the bucket,

Yet, Hera called me with delicate voice and profound:

L.

"'Paris, give me the prize, and thou shalt rule

O'er many noble people groups, all over,

From them that till the dark and disintegrating plain,

Where the sweet waters of Aegyptus coast,

To those that on the Northern walks ride,

Also, the Ceteians, and the chaste men

That round the rising-spot of Morn stand,

And every one of the tenants in the Asian fen.

LI.

"'Furthermore, I will cherish reasonable Ilios as I love

Argos and rich Mycenae, that doth crowd

Profound abundance; and I will make you lord above

100 people groups; men will call you ruler

In tongues thou know'st not; thou shalt be venerated

With penance, just like the Gods divine,

If by some stroke of good luck thou shrivel express a little word,

Furthermore, say the prize of perfection is mine.'

LII.

"Then, at that point, as I questioned, similar to an abrupt fire

Of silver came Athene, and methought

Seeing her, how dignified, as she came,

That faint wood to a fragrant fane was fashioned;

So unadulterated the warlike lady seem'd, that nothing

Yet, her own voice telling made me raise

Mine eyes to see her excellence, who besought

In briefest words the guerdon of all commendation.

LIII.

"She spake: 'Nor abundance nor crowns are in my gift;

Yet, astuteness, however the eyes that look a remote place,

Yet, fortitude, and the soul that is quick

To cut her way through every one of the influxes of war;

Perseverance that the Fates can never damage;

These, and my caring companionship,— these are thine,

What's more, these will direct you, unflinching as a star,

In the event that thou hast eyes to realize the prize is mine.'

LIV.

"Last, in a stunning fog of blushing fire,

Came Aphrodite through the woodland dell,

The sovereign of all pleasure and all longing,

More reasonable than when her stripped foot she laid

On the visually impaired simple's wild wave that sank dismay'd,

What time the ocean developed smoother than a lake;

I was too glad to possibly be sore apprehensive.

What's more, similar to a melody her voice was the point at which she spake:

LV.

"'Goodness Paris, what is power? Tantalus

What's more, Sisyphus were rulers quite a while past,

Be that as it may, presently they lie in the Lake Dolorous,

The slopes of misery are loud with their burden;

Ay, quick the tides of Empire recurring pattern,

Also, that is immediately lost was not really won,

As Ilios herself o'erwell knew

At the point when high dividers help'd not King Laomedon.

LVI.

"'Furthermore, what are strength and fortitude? for the kid

Of powerful Zeus, the resilient man Herakles,

Knew numerous days and wickedness, ere men heaped

The fire in Oeta, where he got his straightforwardness

In death, where every one of the ills of valiant men stop.

Nay, Love I proffer you; past the salt water

Of the multitude of flows of the Western oceans,

The most attractive lady on the planet is thine!'

LVII.

"She spake, and contacted the prize, and all became faint

I heard no voice of anger'd Deity,

Be that as it may, round me did the night air faint and swim,

Also, when I waken'd, lo! the sun was high,

Also, in that spot loathsome did I lie,

Where Agelaus tracked down the stripped kid;

Then, at that point with quick foot I did emerge and fly

Forward from the deeps of that captivated wild.

LVIII.

"And down I sped to Ilios, down the dell
Where, years agone, the white bull guided me,
And through green boughs beheld where foam'd and fell
The merry waters of the Western sea;
Of Love the sweet birds sang from sky and tree,
And swift I reach'd the haven and the shore,
And call'd my mariners, and follow'd free
Where Love might lead across the waters hoar.

LIX.

"Three days with fair winds ran we, then we drave
Before the North that made the long waves swell
Round Malea; but hardly from the wave
We 'scaped at Pylos, Nestor's citadel;
And there the son of Neleus loved us well,
And brought us to the high prince, Diocles,
Who led us hither, and it thus befell
That here, below thy roof, we sit at ease."

LX.

Then all men gave the stranger thanks and praise,
And Menelaus for red wine bade call;
And the sun fell, and dark were all the ways;
Then maidens set forth braziers in the hall,
And heap'd them high with lighted brands withal;
But Helen pass'd, as doth the fading day
Pass from the world, and softly left them all
Loud o'er their wine amid the twilight grey.

LXI.

So night drew on with rain, nor yet they ceased
Within the hall to drink the gleaming wine,
And late they pour'd the last cup of the feast,
To Argus-bane, the Messenger divine;
And last, 'neath torches tall that smoke and shine,
The maidens strew'd the beds with purple o'er,
That Diocles and Paris might recline
All night, beneath the echoing corridor.

Part 2
THE SPELL OF APHRODITE

The coming of Aphrodite, and how she told Helen that she must depart in company with Paris, but promised withal that Helen, having fallen into a deep sleep, should awake forgetful of her old life, and ignorant of her shame, and blameless of those evil deeds that the Goddess thrust upon her.

I.

Now in the upper chamber o'er the gate
Lay Menelaus on his carven bed,
And swift and sudden as the stroke of Fate
A deep sleep fell upon his weary head.
But the soft-wingèd God with wand of lead
Came not near Helen; wistful did she lie,
Till dark should change to grey, and grey to red,
And golden thronèd Morn sweep o'er the sky.

II.

Slow pass'd the weighty evening: like one who fears

The progression of homicide, she lies shuddering,

In the event that any cry of the night bird she hears;

What's more, strains her eyes to check some horrendous thing,

Assuming however the blinds of the window swing,

Stirr'd by the breath of night, and still she sobbed

As she were not the girl of a lord,

Furthermore, no solid ruler, her master, next to her rested.

III.

Presently in that hour, the people who watch the evening,

Shepherds and anglers, and they that handle

Unusual expressions and look for their spells in the star-light,

Observed a wonder in the ocean and sky,

For every one of the influxes of the relative multitude of oceans that murmur

Between the waterways of Hellé and the Nile,

Flush'd with a fire of silver abruptly,

From delicate Cythera to the Cyprian isle.

IV.

Also, Hesperus, the most considerate star of paradise,

That bringeth everything great, wax'd pale, and straight

There fell a glimmer of white dangerous levin

Among the shining waters forsaken;

The lights of ocean and sky did blend and mate

Furthermore, change to ruddy fire, and thus flew

The exquisite Queen of Love that goes to loathe,

Like summer lightnings 'twixt the ocean and sky.

V.

Also, presently the nook of Helen fill'd with light,

Also, presently she knew what she dreaded

Was close upon her (for the dark of night

Doth consume like fire, whene'er the Gods are close);

Then, at that point sparkled like fire each rudder and safeguard and lance

That hung inside the office of the King,

In any case, he,— however all the thicket as day was clear,—

Dozed as they rest that know no arousing.

VI.

Be that as it may, Helen leap'd from her reasonable carven bed

As some tortured thing that dread makes striking,

Furthermore, on the ground she beat her brilliant head

Furthermore, pray'd with harsh moanings complex.

However realized that she would never move the virus

Heart of the beautiful Goddess, remaining there,

Her feet upon a little cloud, a crease

Of silver cloud about her chest uncovered.

VII.

So stood Queen Aphrodite, as she stands

Unaffected in her splendid chateau, when to no end

Some bare lady extends powerless hands

Also, shifts the enchantment wheel, and consumes the grain,

Furthermore, can't win her darling back once more,

Nor her old heart of calm any more,

Where twilight floods the faint Sicilian primary,

Also, the cool wavelets break along the shore.

VIII.

Then, at that point Helen stopped unavailing petition,

What's more, rose and confronted the Goddess consistently,

Till even the giggling adoring woman reasonable

Half shrank before the annoyance of her eye,

What's more, Helen cried with a surpassing cry,

"For what reason does Zeus live, in the event that we to be sure should be

Close to dismal crown jewels of fate,

What's more, captives of an adulteress like you?

IX.

"What wither thou with me, paramour of all misfortune?

Say, shrivel thou bear me to another land

Where thou hast different sweethearts? Rise and go

Where dim the pine trees upon Ida stand,

For there did one unloose thy support band;

Or on the other hand look for the woods where Adonis drained,

Or on the other hand meander, meander on the yellow sand,

Where thy first sweetheart strew'd thy marriage bed.

X.

"Ok, thy first darling! who is first or last

Of men and divine beings, unnumber'd and anonymous?

Darling by sweetheart in the race is pass'd,

Darling by sweetheart, pariah and embarrassed.

Goodness, thou of many names, and evil celebrated!

What shrink thou with me? What must I persevere

Whose spirit, for all thy make, is rarely restrained?

Whose heart, for all thy wiles, is ever unadulterated?

XI.

"View, my heart is cleaner than the tuft

Upon the pure pinions of the swan,

What's more, thou wither smear and stain it with the smoke

Of all thy contemptuous desires Idalian.

My name will be a murmuring that a man

Will grin to talk, and ladies revile and disdain,

Also, on my young kid will come a boycott,

And all my grandiose home be barren.

XII.

"Is it thy will that like a golden cup
From lip to lip of heroes I must go,
And be but as a banner lifted up,
To beckon where the winds of war may blow?
Have I not seen fair Athens in her woe,
And all her homes aflame from sea to sea,
When my fierce brothers wrought her overthrow
Because Athenian Theseus carried me—

XIII.

"Me, in my bloomless youth, a maiden child,
From Artemis' pure altars and her fane,
And bare me, with Pirithous the wild
To rich Aphidna? Many a man was slain,
And wet with blood the fair Athenian plain,
And fired was many a goodly temple then,

But fire nor blood can purify the stain
Nor make my name reproachless among men."

XIV.

Then Helen ceased, her passion like a flame
That slays the thing it lives by, blazed and fell,
As faint as waves at dawn, though fierce they came,
By night to storm some rocky citadel;
For Aphrodite answer'd,—like a spell
Her voice makes strength of mortals pass away,—
"Dost thou not know that I have loved thee well,
And never loved thee better than to-day?

XV.

"Behold, thine eyes are wet, thy cheeks are wan,
Yet art thou born of an immortal sire,
The child of Nemesis and of the Swan;
Thy veins should run with ichor and with fire.
Yet this is thy delight and thy desire,
To love a mortal lord, a mortal child,
To live, unpraised of lute, unhymn'd of lyre,
As any woman pure and undefiled.

XVI.

"Thou art the toy of Gods, an instrument
Wherewith all mortals shall be plagued or blest,
Even at my pleasure; yea, thou shalt be bent
This way and that, howe'er it like me best:
And following thee, as tides the moon, the West
Shall flood the Eastern coasts with waves of war,

And thy vex'd soul shall scarcely be at rest,
Even in the havens where the deathless are.

XVII.

"The instruments of men are blind and dumb,
And this one gift I give thee, to be blind
And heedless of the thing that is to come,
And ignorant of that which is behind;
Bearing an innocent forgetful mind
In each new fortune till I visit thee
And stir thy heart, as lightning and the wind
Bear fire and tumult through a sleeping sea.

XVIII.

"Thou shalt forget Hermione; forget
Thy lord, thy lofty palace, and thy kin;
Thy hand within a stranger's shalt thou set,
And follow him, nor deem it any sin;
And many a strange land wand'ring shalt thou win,
And thou shalt come to an unhappy town,
And twenty long years shalt thou dwell therein,
Before the Argives mar its towery crown.

XIX.

"And of thine end I speak not, but thy name,—
Thy name which thou lamentest,—that shall be
A song in all men's speech, a tongue of flame
Between the burning lips of Poesy;
And the nine daughters of Mnemosyne,
With Prince Apollo, leader of the nine,

Shall make thee deathless in their minstrelsy!
Yea, for thou shalt outlive the race divine,

XX.

"The race of Gods, for like the children of men

We Gods have yet our season, and pass by;

Also, Cronos pass'd, and Uranus, and afterward

Will Zeus and every one of his kids completely

Pass, and new Gods be conceived, and rule, and kick the
bucket,—

In any case, you will sweethearts love evermore

What Gods soe'er usurp the changeful sky,

Or on the other hand dance to the irremeable shore.

XXI.

"Presently rest and dream not, rest the difficult day through,

Also, the brief watches of the mid year night,

And afterward go forward in the midst of the blossoms and dew,

Where the red rose of Dawn outburns the white.

Then, at that point shalt thou become familiar with my leniency
and my strength

Between the languid lily and the rose;

There shalt thou spell the importance of pleasure,

Furthermore, know such joy as a Goddess knows!"

XXII.

Then, at that point Sleep came skimming from the Lemnian isle,

Furthermore, over Helen crush'd his poppy crown,

Her delicate tops waver'd for a brief period,

Then, at that point on her carven bed she laid her down,

Furthermore, Sleep, the blanket of lord and jokester,

Kind Sleep the best, close much the same as Death,

Held her as close as Death doth men that suffocate,

So close that none may hear her internal breath—

XXIII.

So close no man may tell she was not dead!

And afterward the Goddess took her zone,— where lies

All her charm, love and lustihead,

Also, the happy talk that overwhelms the astute,

Also, beauty the very Gods may not disdain,

Also, sweet Desire that doth the entire world move,—

Also, therewith touch'd she Helen's resting eyes

Also, made her exquisite as the Queen of Love.

XXIV.

Then, at that point giggling cherishing Aphrodite went

To far Idalia, over land and ocean,

Also, scant the fragrant cedar-branches twisted

Underneath her strides, faring gently;

Also, in Idalia the Graces three

Blessed her with oil ambrosial,—

So to her home in Sidon wended she

To taunt the petitions of darlings when they call.

XXV.

And the entire day the incense and the smoke

Lifted, and fell, and delicate and gradually roll'd,

Furthermore, numerous a psalm and melodic got up

Between the mainstays of her place of gold,

Also, rose-crown'd young ladies, and reasonable young men
material stoled,

Forfeited her fragrant courts inside,

Also, in dim churches fashioned rituals complex

The caring blessing of the Queen to win.

XXVI.

Yet, Menelaus, waking unexpectedly,

Seen the first light was white, the day was close,

Furthermore, rose, and kiss'd reasonable Helen; no decent bye

He spake, and never mark'd a fallen tear,—

Men know not when they part for some a year,—

He grasp'd a bronze-shod spear in one or the other hand,

Furthermore, happily went forward to drive the deer,

With Paris, through the dewy morning land.

XXVII.

So up the lofty sides of Taygetus

They fared, and to the breezy hollows came,

While from the floods of profound Oceanus

The sun emerged, and on the fields blazed;

Also, through wet knolls the huntsmen drave the game,

Also, with them Paris sway'd a gray lance,

Weighty, and long, and shod with bronze to tame

The mountain-abiding goats and woodland deer.

XXVIII.

Presently in a brush a powerful pig there lay,

For through the limbs the wet breezes won't ever blow,

Nor lit the brilliant sun on it with his beam,

Nor downpour may puncture the woven branches through,

Yet, leaves had fallen profound the nest to toss:

Then, at that point questing of the dogs and men's foot-fall

Stirred the hog, and forward he sprang to see,

With eyes that burn'd, under control, before them all.

XXIX.

Then, at that point Paris was quick to surge on him,

With skewer up high in his solid hand to destroy,

Furthermore, through the beast penetrated the point; and faint

The fire fell in his eyes, and everything his strength

With his last cry went forward; neglecting battle,

Failing to remember strength, he fell, and happily then, at that point

They gather'd round, and managed him aright;

Then, at that point left his body with the serving men.

XXX.

Presently birds were long conscious, that with their cry

Were wont to arouse Helen; and the dew

Where fell the sun upon the grass was dry,

And all the late spring land was happy once more;

Furthermore, ladies' strides rang the royal residence through,

Also, with their strides ringed their glad melody,

Also, one to other cried, "A wonder new

That delicate wing'd Sleep hath held the Queen so long!"

XXXI.

Then, at that point Phylo brought the kid Hermione,

Also, close unto her mom's side she crawled,

Also, o'er her god-like excellence tumbled she,

Reprimanding her pleasantly that so late she rested,

Jabbering still a happy curl she kept;

In any case, similar to a lady hardened underneath her cover

Lay Helen; till the little youngster fear'd and sobbed,

What's more, ran, and to her medical attendants cried
resoundingly.

XXXII.

Then, at that point came the ladies rapidly, and in fear

Gather'd round Helen, however may nothing profit

To wake her; moveless as a lady dead

That Artemis hath killed, yet nowise pale,

She lay; yet Aethra started the cry,

And every one of the ladies with miserable voice answered,

Who deem'd her pass'd unto the poplar vale

Wherein doth fear Persephone withstand.

XXXIII.

Ok! gradually pass'd the hopeless day

In the rich house that late was brimming proudly;

Then, at that point the sun fell, and every one of the ways were
dim,

Furthermore, Menelaus from the mountain-side

Came, and through royal residence entryways all open wide

Rang the wild requiem that advised him of the thing

That Helen, that the Queen had peculiarly passed on.

Then, at that point on his edge fell he stooping,

XXXIV.

What's more, provided reason to feel ambiguous about the
residue his yellow hair,

Furthermore, however that Paris leap'd and held his hand,

His tracker's blade would he have clutch'd, and there

Had killed himself, to follow to that land

Where bounce the apparitions of men, a shadowy band

That have no more joy, no more craving,

At the point when the tissue hath burn'd down like a brand,

Drench'd by the dull wine on the memorial service fire:

XXXV.

So on the ashen threshold lay the king,
And all within the house was chill and drear;
The women watchers gather'd in a ring
About the bed of Helen and her bier;
And much had they to tell, and much to hear,
Of happy queens and fair, untimely dead,—
Such joy they took amid their evil cheer,—
While the low thunder muttered overhead.

Part 3
THE FLIGHT OF HELEN

The flight of Helen and Paris from Lacedaemon, and of what things befell them in their voyaging, and how they came to Troy.

I.

The grey Dawn's daughter, rosy Morn awoke
In old Tithonus' arms, and suddenly
Let harness her swift steeds beneath the yoke,
And drave her shining chariot through the sky.
Then men might see the flocks of Thunder fly,
All gold and rose, the azure pastures through,
What time the lark was carolling on high
Above the gardens drench'd with rainy dew.

II.

But Aphrodite sent a slumber deep
On all in the King's palace, young and old,
And one by one the women fell asleep,—
Their lamentable tales left half untold,—
Before the dawn, when folk wax weak and cold,
But Helen waken'd with the shining morn,
Forgetting quite her sorrows manifold,
And light of heart as was the day new-born.

III.

She had no memory of unhappy things,
She knew not of the evil days to come,
Forgotten were her ancient wanderings,
And as Lethaean waters wholly numb
The sense of spirits in Elysium,

That no remembrance may their bliss alloy,
Even so the rumour of her days was dumb,
And all her heart was ready for new joy.

IV.

The young day knows not of an elder dawn,
Joys of old noons, old sorrows of the night,
And so from Helen was the past withdrawn,
Her lord, her child, her home forgotten quite,
Lost in the marvel of a new delight:
She was as one who knows he shall not die,
When earthly colours melt into the bright
Pure splendour of his immortality.

V.

Then Helen rose, and all her body fair
She bath'd in the spring water, pure and cold,
And with her hand bound up her shining hair
And clothed her in the raiment that of old
Athene wrought with marvels manifold,
A bridal gift from an immortal hand,
And all the front was clasp'd with clasps of gold,
And for the girdle was a golden band.

VI.

Next from her upper chamber silently
Went Helen, moving like a morning dream.
She did not know the golden roof, the high
Walls, and the shields that on the pillars gleam,
Only she heard the murmur of the stream

That waters all the garden's wide expanse,
This song, and cry of singing birds, did seem
To guide her feet as music guides the dance.

VII.

The music attracted her on to the happy air

From forward the office of captivated demise,

Furthermore, lo! the world was waking all over;

The breeze passed by, a cool flavorful breath,

Like what in the nurseries wandereth,

The brilliant nurseries of the Hesperides,

Also, in its tune incomprehensible things it saith,

The bunch wonders of the pixie oceans.

VIII.

So through the patio to the nursery close

Went Helen, where she heard the mumbling

Of water 'twixt the lily and the rose;

For in this manner doth a twofold wellspring spring.

To one stream do the ladies pitchers bring

By Menelaus' entryways, at close of day;

The other through the nearby doth sparkle and sing,

Then, at that point to the quick Eurotas armadas away.

IX.

What's more, Helen put her downward on the grass,

Furthermore, pluck'd the little daisies white and red,

Furthermore, toss'd them where the running waters pass,

To watch them hustling from the wellspring head,

Furthermore, whirl'd regarding where little streams dispread;

Furthermore, still with happy birds the nursery rang,

Furthermore, wed, wed, in their melody they said,

Or thereabouts do house cleaners decipher that they sang.

X.

Then, at that point stoop'd she down, and watch'd the precious stone stream,

Furthermore, fishes balancing where the waters ran,

Furthermore, lo! upon the glass a brilliant glimmer,

Also, purple as of robes Sidonian,

Then, at that point, unexpected turning, she observed a man,

That bowed adjacent to her; as her own face reasonable

Was his, and o'er his shoulders for a range

Fell the brilliant braids of his yellow hair.

XI.

Then, at that point either look'd on other with astonish

As each had seen a God; for no drawn-out period of time

They marvell'd, however as in the first of days,

The first of men and house keepers did meet and grin,

What's more, Aphrodite did their hearts flabbergast,

So hands met hands, lips, with no word said

Were they captivated 'neath that verdant passageway,

Furthermore, quietly were woo'd, betroth'd, and marry.

XII.

Ok, gradually did their quietness wake to words

That scant had a greater amount of importance than the melody

Pour'd forward of the incalculable birds

That fill the royal residence cultivates the entire day;

So honest, so uninformed about wrong,

Was she, so glad each in other's eyes,

Subsequently created the powerful Goddess that is solid,

Indeed, even to make nothing the intelligence of the savvy.

XIII.

Presently amidst that captivated spot

Right readily had they linger'd the entire day through,

Furthermore, took care of their adoration upon one another's face,

However, Aphrodite had a guidance new,

Also, quietly to Paris' side she drew,

In pretense of Aethra, murmuring that the day

Pass'd on, while his boat paused, and his team

Fretful, in the limited Gythian sound.

XIV.

For yonder had she brought them by her expertise;

However, Helen saw her not,— nay, who can see

A Goddess come or conflict with her will?

Then, at that point Paris whisper'd, "Come, ah, Love, with me!

Go to a shore past the desolate ocean;

There doth the marriage crown anticipate thy head,

Also, there will all the land be happy of you!"

Then, at that point, similar to a youngster, she follow'd where he drove.

XV.

For, similar to a youngster's her delicate heart was happy.

So through the yard pass'd they to the door;

Furthermore, even there, as Aphrodite bade,

The horses of Paris and the chariots pause;

Then, at that point to the well-created vehicle he drove her straight,

Also, got a handle on the sparkling whip and brilliant rein,

What's more, quick they drave until the day was late

By clear Eurotas through the productive plain.

XVI.

Be that as it may, presently inside the lobbies the wizardry rest

Was broken, and men looked for them all over the place;

However Aphrodite cast a cloud so profound

Regarding their chariot none may see them there.

Furthermore, unusually did they hear the trumpets blast,

Furthermore, commotion of dashing wheels; yet saw they nothing:

Then, at that point kicked the bucket the sounds upon the far off air,

Also, safe they won the safe house that they looked for.

XVII.

Underneath a green precipice, underneath the down,

Where quick Eurotas blends with the ocean,

There climb'd the dim dividers of a little town,

The tired waters wash'd it lazily,

For storms in that safe house probably won't be.

The isle across the gulf monitored all,

Also, the abrasive breezes that wander the sea free

Broke and were broken on the rough divider.

XVIII.

Then, at that point Paris did a state of chasing blow,

Nor yet the sound had kicked the bucket upon the slope

When round the isle they saw a red fore,

Also, paddles that flash'd into that asylum still,

The rowers twisting forward with a will,

Also, quick their dark boat to the shelter side

They brought, and steer'd her in with goodly ability,

Also, uncovered on board the abnormal Achaean lady.

XIX.

Presently while the quick boat through the waters clave,

All cheerful things that in the waters abide,

Emerged and gamboll'd on the lustrous wave,

Also, Nereus drove them with his sounding shell:

Yea, the ocean sprites, their moves weaving admirably,

In the green water gave them welcoming free.

Ok, long light linger'd, late the obscurity fell,

That evening, upon the isle of Cranaë!

XX.

Furthermore, Hymen shook his fragrant light on high,

Till every one of its influxes of smoke and tongues of fire,

Like billows of ruddy gold fulfill'd the sky;

And every one of the Nereids from the waters came,

Every lady with a melodic sweet name;

Doris, and Doto, and Amphithoë;

Furthermore, their sharp wedding melody of adoration and disgrace

Made music in the quietness of the ocean.

XXI.

For this resembled that evening of summer climate,

At the point when mortal men and ladies unafraid,

Furthermore, woods sprites, and timberland divine beings together,

Do venerate Pan in the long nightfall clear.

What's more, Artemis this one night saves the deer,

What's more, every cavern and dell, and each forest

Is happy with singing delicate and glad cheer,

With giggling, and with dalliance, and with adoration.

* * *

XXII.

Presently when the brilliant thronèd Dawn emerged

To arouse divine beings and humans out of rest,

Sovereign Aphrodite sent the breeze that blows

From pixie nurseries of the Western profound.

The sails are spread, the paddles of Paris jump

Past numerous a headland, numerous a spooky fane:

What's more, joyfully all from one isle to another they clear

O'er the wet ways across the infertile plain.

XXIII.

By numerous an island fortress, and numerous a safe house

They sped, and numerous a jam-packed arms stockpile:

They saw the loves of Gods and men engraven

On friezes of Astarte's sanctuary divider.

They heard that old shepherd Proteus call

His rush from forward the green and tumbling lea,

Also, saw white Thetis with her ladies all

Clear up to high Olympus from the ocean.

XXIV.

They saw the vain and fatigued work of men,

The boats that success the rich man all he aches for;

They pass'd the red-prow'd barks Egyptian,

Furthermore, heard a remote place the groaning of the slaves

Confined in obscurity hot hold underneath the waves;

Also, perfect the Sardanian armadas among

They sail'd; by men that sow the ocean with graves,

Bearing dark destiny to people of outsider tongue.

XXV.

Then, at that point the entire day a moving haze of smoke

Would hold tight as far as possible, weak and far,

Yet, during that time the reference point fire upbroke

From some rich island-town begirt with war;

And this load of things could neither make nor deface

The delight of sweethearts meandering, however they

Sped joyfully, and indiscreet of the star

That hung o'er their happy sanctuary, far away.

XXVI.

The fisher-sentinel upon the height
Watch'd them with vacant eyes, and little knew
They bore the fate of Troy; to him the bright
Plashed waters, with the silver shining through
When tunny shoals came cruising in the blue,
Was more than Love that doth the world unmake;
And listless gazed he as the gulls that flew
And shriek'd and chatter'd in the vessel's wake.

XXVII.

So the wind drave them, and the waters bare
Across the great green plain unharvested,
Till through an after-glow they knew the fair
Faint rose of snow on distant Ida's head.
And swifter then the joyous oarsmen sped;
But night was ended, and the waves were fire
Beneath the fleet feet of a dawning red
Or ere they won the land of their desire.

XXVIII.

Now when the folk about the haven knew
The scarlet prow of Paris, swift they ran
And the good ship within the haven drew,
And merrily their welcoming began.
But none the face of Helen dared to scan;
Their bold eyes fell before they had their fill,
For all men deem'd her that Idalian
Who loved Anchises on the lonely hill.

XXIX.

But when her sweet smile and her gentleness
And her kind speech had won them from dismay,
They changed their minds, and 'gan the Gods to bless
Who brought to Ilios that happy day.
And all the folk fair Helen must convey,
Crown'd like a bride, and clad with flame-hued pall,
Through the rich plain, along the water-way
Right to the great gates of the Ilian wall.

XXX.

And through the vines they pass'd, where old and young
Had no more heed of the glad vintaging,
But all unpluck'd the purple clusters hung,
Nor more of Linus did the minstrel sing,
For he and all the folk were following,
Wine-stain'd and garlanded, in merry bands,
Like men when Dionysus came as king,
And led his revel from the sun-burnt lands,

XXXI.

So from afar the music and the shout
Roll'd up to Ilios and the Scaean gate,
And at the sound the city folk came out
And bore sweet Helen—such a fairy weight
As none might deem the burden of Troy's fate—
Across the threshold of the town, and all
Flock'd with her, where King Priam sat in state,
Girt by his elders, on the Ilian wall.

XXXII.

No man but knew him by his crown of gold,
And golden-studded sceptre, and his throne;
Ay, strong he seem'd as those great kings of old,
Whose image is eternal on the stone
Won from the dust that once was Babylon;
But kind of mood was he withal, and mild,
And when his eyes on Argive Helen shone,
He loved her as a father doth a child.

XXXIII.

Round him were set his peers, as Panthous,
Antenor, and Agenor, hardly grey,
Scarce touch'd as yet with age, nor garrulous
As are cicalas on a sunny day:
Such might they be when years had slipp'd away,
And made them over-weak for war or joy,
Content to watch the Leaguer as it lay
Beside the ships, beneath the walls of Troy.

XXXIV.

Then Paris had an easy tale to tell,
Which then might win upon men's wond'ring ears,
Who deem'd that Gods with mortals deign to dwell,
And that the water of the West enspheres
The happy Isles that know not Death nor tears;
Yea, and though monsters do these islands guard,
Yet men within their coasts had dwelt for years
Uncounted, with a strange love for reward.

XXXV.

And there had Paris ventured: so said he,—
Had known the Sirens' song, and Circe's wile;
And in a cove of that Hesperian sea
Had found a maiden on a lonely isle;
A sacrifice, if so men might beguile
The wrath of some beast-god they worshipp'd there,
But Paris, 'twixt the sea and strait defile,
Had slain the beast, and won the woman fair.

XXXVI.

Then while the happy people cried "Well done,"
And Priam's heart was melted by the tale—
For Paris was his best-belovèd son—
Came a wild woman, with wet eyes, and pale
Sad face, men look'd on when she cast her veil,
Not gladly; and none mark'd the thing she said,
Yet must they hear her long and boding wail
That follow'd still, however fleet they fled.

XXXVII.

She was the priestess of Apollo's fane,
Cassandra, and the God of prophecy
Spurr'd her to speak and rent her! but in vain
She toss'd her wasted arms against the sky,
And brake her golden circlet angrily,
And shriek'd that they had brought within the gate
Helen, a serpent at their hearts to lie!
Helen, a hell of people, king, and state!

XXXVIII.

But ere the God had left her; ere she fell
And foam'd among her maidens on the ground,
The air was ringing with a merry swell
Of flute, and pipe, and every sweetest sound,
In Aphrodite's fane, and all around
Were roses toss'd beneath the glimmering green
Of that high roof, and Helen there was crown'd
The Goddess of the Trojans, and their Queen.

Part 4
THE DEATH OF CORYTHUS

How Helen was made an outcast by the Trojan women, and how Œnone, the old love of Paris, sent her son Corythus to him as her messenger, and how Paris slew him unwittingly; and of the curses of Œnone, and the coming of the Argive host against Troy.

I.

For long in Troia was there peace and mirth,
The pleasant hours still passing one by one;
And Helen joy'd at each fresh morning's birth,
And almost wept at setting of the sun,
For sorrow that the happy day was done;
Nor dream'd of years when she should hate the light,
And mourn afresh for every day begun,
Nor fare abroad save shamefully by night.

II.

And Paris was not one to backward cast
A fearful glance; nor pluck sour fruits of sin,
Half ripe; but seized all pleasures while they last,
Nor boded evil ere ill days begin.
Nay, nor lamented much when caught therein,
In each adventure always finding joy,
And hopeful still through waves of war to win
By strength of Hector, and the star of Troy.

III.

Now as the storms drive white sea-birds afar
Within green upland glens to seek for rest,
So rumours pale of an approaching war

99

Were blown across the islands from the west:
For Agamemnon summon'd all the best
From towns and tribes he ruled, and gave command
That free men all should gather at his hest
Through coasts and islets of the Argive land.

IV.

Sidonian merchant-men had seen the fleet
Black war-galleys that sped from town to town;
Had heard the hammers of the bronze-smiths beat
The long day through, and when the sun went down;
And thin, said they, would show the leafy crown
On many a sacred mountain-peak in spring,
For men had fell'd the pine-trees tall and brown
To fashion them curved ships for seafaring.

V.

And still the rumour grew; for heralds came,
Old men from Argos, bearing holy boughs,
Demanding great atonement for the shame
And sore despite done Menelaus' house;
But homeward soon they turn'd their scarlet prows,
And all their weary voyaging was vain;
For Troy had bound herself with awful vows
To cleave to Helen till the walls were ta'en.

VI.

And now, like swallows ere the winter weather,
The women in shrill groups were gathering,
With eager tongues still communing together,

And many a taunt at Helen would they fling,
Ay, through her innocence she felt the sting,
And shamed was now her gentle face and sweet,
For e'en the children evil songs would sing
To mock her as she hasted down the street.

VII.

Also the men who worshipp'd her of old
As she had been a goddess from above,
Gazed at her now with lustful eyes and bold,
As she were naught but Paris' light-o'-love;
And though in truth they still were proud enough,
Of that fair gem in their old city set,
Yet well she knew that wanton word and scoff
Went round the camp-fire when the warriors met.

VIII.

There came a certain holiday when Troy
Was wont to send her noble matrons all,
Young wives and old, with clamour and with joy,
To clothe Athene in her temple hall,
And robe her in a stately broider'd pall.
But now they drove fair Helen from their train,
"Better," they scream'd, "to cast her from the wall,
Than mock the Gods with offerings in vain."

IX.

One joy she had, that Paris yet was true,
Ay, fickle Paris, true unto the end;
And in the court of Ilios were two

Kind hearts, still eager Helen to defend,
And help and comfort in all need to lend:—
The gentle Hector with soft speech and mild,
And the old king that ever was her friend,
And loved her as a father doth his child.

X.

These, though they knew not all, these blamed her not,
But cast the heavy burden on the God,
Whose wrath, they deem'd, had verily waxed hot
Against the painful race on earth that trod,
And in God's hand was Helen but the rod
To scourge a people that, in unknown wise,
Had vex'd the far Olympian abode
With secret sin or stinted sacrifice.

* * * * * *

XI.

The days grew into months, and months to years,
And still the Argive army did delay,
Till folk in Troia half forgot their fears,
And almost as of old were glad and gay;
And men and maids on Ida dared to stray,
But Helen dwelt within her inmost room,
And there from dawning to declining day,
Wrought at the patient marvels of her loom.

XII.

Yet even there in peace she might not be:
There was a nymph, Œnone, in the hills,
The daughter of a River-God was she,
Of Cebren,—that the mountain silence fills
With murmur'd music, for the countless rills
Of Ida meet him, dancing to the plain,—
Her Paris wooed, yet ignorant of ills,
Among the shepherd's huts, nor wooed in vain.

XIII.

Nay, Summer often found them by the fold
In these glad days, ere Paris was a king,
And oft the Autumn, in his car of gold,
Had pass'd them, merry at the vintaging:
And scarce they felt the breath of the white wing
Of Winter, in the cave where they would lie
On beds of heather by the fire, till Spring
Should crown them with her buds in passing by.

XIV.

For elbow-deep their flowery bed was strown
With fragrant leaves and with crush'd asphodel,
And sweetly still the shepherd-pipe made moan,
And many a tale of Love they had to tell,—
How Daphnis loved the strange, shy maiden well,
And how she loved him not, and how he died,
And oak-trees moan'd his dirge, and blossoms fell
Like tears from lindens by the water-side!

XV.

But colder, fleeter than the Winter's wing,
Time pass'd; and Paris changed, and now no more
Œnone heard him on the mountain sing,
Not now she met him in the forest hoar.
Nay, but she knew that on an alien shore
An alien love he sought; yet was she strong
To live, who deem'd that even as of yore
In days to come might Paris love her long.

XVI.

For dark Œnone from her Father drew
A power beyond all price; the gift to deal
With wounded men, though now the dreadful dew
Of Death anoint them, and the secret seal
Of Fate be set on them; these might she heal;
And thus Œnone trusted still to save
Her lover at the point of death, and steal
His life from Helen, and the amorous grave.

XVII.

And she had borne, though Paris knew it not,
A child, fair Corythus, to be her shame,
And still she mused, whenas her heart was hot,
"He hath no child by that Achaean dame:"
But when her boy unto his manhood came,
Then sorer yet Œnone did repine,
And bade him "fare to Ilios, and claim
Thy father's love, and all that should be thine!"

XVIII.

Therewith a golden bodkin from her hair
She drew, and from a green-tress'd birchen tree
She pluck'd a strip of smooth white bark and fair,
And many signs and woful gravèd she,
A message of the evil things to be.
Then deftly closed the birch-bark, fold on fold,
And bound the tokens well and cunningly,
Three times and four times, with a thread of gold.

XIX.

"Give these to Argive Helen's hand," she cried:
And so embraced her child, and with no fear
Beheld him leaping down the mountain-side,
Like a king's son that goes to hunt the deer,
Clad softly, and in either hand a spear,
With two swift-footed hounds that follow'd him,
So leap'd he down the grassy slopes and sheer,
And won the precinct of the forest dim.

XX.

He trod that ancient path his sire had trod,
Far, far below he saw the sea, the town;
He moved as light as an immortal god,
For mansions in Olympus gliding down.
He left the shadow of the forest brown,
And through the shallow waters did he cross,
And stood, ere twilight fell, within the crown
Of towers, the sacred keep of Ilios.

XXI.

Now folk that mark'd him hasting deem'd that he
Had come to tell the host was on its way,
As one that from the hills had seen the sea
Beclouded with the Danaan array,
So straight to Paris' house with no delay
They led him, and did eagerly await
Within the forecourt, in the twilight grey,
To hear some certain message of their fate.

XXII.

Now Paris was asleep upon his bed
Tired with a listless day; but all along
The palace chambers Corythus was led,
And still he heard a music, shrill and strong,
That seem'd to clamour of an old-world wrong,
And hearts a long time broken; last they came
To Helen's bower, the fountain of the song
That cried so loud against an ancient shame.

XXIII.

And Helen fared before a mighty loom,
And sang, and cast her shuttle wrought of gold,
And forth unto the utmost secret room
The wave of her wild melody was roll'd;
And still she fashion'd marvels manifold,
Strange shapes of fish and serpent, bear and swan,
The loves of the immortal Gods of old,
Wherefrom the peoples of the world began.

XXIV.

Now Helen met the stranger graciously
With gentle speech, and bade set forth a chair
Well wrought of cedar wood and ivory
That wise Icmalius had fashion'd fair.
But when young Corythus had drunk the rare
Wine of the princes, and had broken bread,
Then Helen took the word, and bade declare
His instant tidings; and he spake and said,

XXV.

"Lady and Queen, I have a secret word,
And bear a token sent to none but thee,
Also I bring message to my Lord
That spoken to another may not be."
Then Helen gave a sign unto her three
Bower-maidens, and they went forth from that place,
Silent they went; and all forebodingly,
They left the man and woman face to face.

XXVI.

Then from his breast the birchen scroll he took
And gave to Helen; and she read therein:
"Oh thou that on those hidden runes dost look,
Hast thou forgotten quite thine ancient sin,
Thy Lord, thy lofty palace, and thy kin,
Even as thy Love forgets the words he spoke
The strong oath broken one weak heart to win,
The lips that kiss'd him, and the heart that broke?

XXVII.

"Nay, but methinks thou shalt not quite forget
The curse wherewith I curse thee till I die;
The tears that on the wood-nymph's cheeks are wet,
Shall burn thy hateful beauty deathlessly,
Nor shall God raise up seed to thee; but I
Have borne thy love this messenger: my son,
Who yet shall make him glad, for Time goes by
And soon shall thine enchantments all be done:

XXVIII.

"Ay, soon 'twixt me and Death must be his choice,
And little in that hour will Paris care
For thy sweet lips, and for thy singing voice,
Thine arms of ivory, thy golden hair.
Nay, me will he embrace, and will not spare,
But bid the folk that hate thee have their joy,
And give thee to the mountain beasts to tear,
Or burn thy body on a tower of Troy."

XXIX.

Even as she read, by Aphrodite's will
The cloud roll'd back from Helen's memory:
She saw the city of the rifted hill,
Fair Lacedaemon, 'neath her mountain high;
She knew the swift Eurotas running by
To mix his sacred waters with the sea,
And from the garden close she heard the cry
Of her beloved child, Hermione.

XXX.

Then instantly the horror of her shame
Fell on her, and she saw the coming years;
Famine, and fire, and plague, and all men's blame,
The wounds of warriors and the women's fears;
And through her heart her sorrow smote like spears,
And in her soul she knew the utmost smart
Of wives left lonely, sires bereaved, the tears
Of maidens desolate, of loves that part.

XXXI.

She drain'd the dregs out of the cup of hate;
The bitterness of sorrow, shame, and scorn;
Where'er the tongues of mortals curse their fate,
She saw herself an outcast and forlorn;
And hating sore the day that she was born,
Down in the dust she cast her golden head,
There with rent raiment and fair tresses torn,
At feet of Corythus she lay for dead.

XXXII.

But Corythus, beholding her sweet face,
And her most lovely body lying low,
Had pity on her grief and on her grace,
Nor heeded now she was his mother's foe,
But did what might be done to ease her woe,
While, as he thought, with death for life she strove,
And loosed the necklet round her neck of snow,
As who that saw had deem'd, with hands of love.

XXXIII.

And there was one that saw: for Paris woke
Half-deeming and half-dreaming that the van
Of the great Argive host had scared the folk,
And down the echoing corridor he ran
To Helen's bower, and there beheld the man
That kneel'd beside his lady lying there:
No word he spake, but drove his sword a span
Through Corythus' fair neck and cluster'd hair.

XXXIV.

Then fell fair Corythus, as falls the tower
An earthquake shaketh from a city's crown,
Or as a tall white fragrant lily-flower
A child hath in the garden trampled down,
Or as a pine-tree in the forest brown,
Fell'd by the sea-rovers on mountain lands,
When they to harry foreign folk are boune,
Taking their own lives in their reckless hands.

XXXV.

But still in Paris did his anger burn,
And still his sword was lifted up to slay,
When, like a lot leap'd forth of Fate's own urn,
He mark'd the graven tokens where they lay,
'Mid Helen's hair in golden disarray,
And looking on them, knew what he had done,
Knew what dire thing had fallen on that day,
Knew how a father's hand had slain a son.

XXXVI.

Then Paris on his face fell grovelling,
And the night gather'd, and the silence grew
Within the darkened chamber of the king.
But Helen rose, and a sad breath she drew,
And her new woes came back to her anew:
Ah, where is he but knows the bitter pain
To wake from dreams, and find his sorrow true,
And his ill life returned to him again!

XXXVII.

She needed none to tell her whence it fell,
The thick red rain upon the marble floor:
She knew that in her bower she might not dwell,
Alone with her own heart for ever more;
No sacrifice, no spell, no priestly lore
Could banish quite the melancholy ghost
Of Corythus; a herald sent before
Them that should die for her, a dreadful host.

XXXVIII.

But slowly Paris raised him from the earth,
And read her face, and knew that she knew all,
No more her eyes, in tenderness or mirth,
Should answer his, in bower or in hall.
Nay, Love had fallen when his child did fall,
The stream Love cannot cross ran 'twixt them red;
No more was Helen his, whate'er befall,
Not though the Goddess drove her to his bed.

XXXIX.

This word he spake, "the Fates are hard on us"—
Then bade the women do what must be done
To the fair body of dead Corythus.
And then he hurl'd into the night alone,
Wailing unto the spirit of his son,
That somewhere in dark mist and sighing wind
Must dwell, nor yet to Hades had it won,
Nor quite had left the world of men behind.

XL.

But wild Œnone by the mountain-path
Saw not her son returning to the wold,
And now was she in fear, and now in wrath
She cried, "He hath forgot the mountain fold,
And goes in Ilios with a crown of gold:"
But even then she heard men's axes smite
Against the beeches slim and ash-trees old,
These ancient trees wherein she did delight.

XLI.

Then she arose and silently as Sleep,
Unseen she follow'd the slow-rolling wain,
Beneath an ashen sky that 'gan to weep,
Too heavy laden with the latter rain;
And all the folk of Troy upon the plain
She found, all gather'd round a funeral pyre,
And thereon lay her son, her darling slain,
The goodly Corythus, her heart's desire!

XLII.

Among the spices and fair robes he lay,
His arm beneath his head, as though he slept.
For so the Goddess wrought that no decay,
No loathly thing about his body crept;
And all the people look'd on him and wept,
And, weeping, Paris lit the pine-wood dry,
And lo, a rainy wind arose and swept
The flame and fragrance far into the sky.

XLIII.

But when the force of flame was burning low,
Then did they drench the pyre with ruddy wine,
And the white bones of Corythus bestow
Within a gold cruse, wrought with many a sign,
And wrapp'd the cruse about with linen fine
And bare it to the tomb: when, lo, the wild
Œnone sprang, with burning eyes divine,
And shriek'd unto the slayer of her child:

XLIV.

"Oh Thou, that like a God art sire and slayer,
That like a God, dost give and take away!
Methinks that even now I hear the prayer
Thou shalt beseech me with, some later day;
When all the world to thy dim eyes grow grey,
And thou shalt crave thy healing at my hand,
Then gladly will I mock, and say thee nay,
And watch thine hours run down like running sand!

XLV.

"Yea, thou shalt die, and leave thy love behind,
And little shall she love thy memory!
But, oh ye foolish people, deaf and blind,
What Death is coming on you from the sea?"
Then all men turned, and lo, upon the lee
Of Tenedos, beneath the driving rain,
The countless Argive ships were racing free,
The wind and oarsmen speeding them amain.

XLVI.

Then from the barrow and the burial,
Back like a bursting torrent all men fled
Back to the city and the sacred wall.
But Paris stood, and lifted not his head.
Alone he stood, and brooded o'er the dead,
As broods a lion, when a shaft hath flown,
And through the strong heart of his mate hath sped,
Then will he face the hunters all alone.

XLVII.

But soon the voice of men on the sea-sand
Came round him; and he turned, and gazed, and lo!
The Argive ships were dashing on the strand:
Then stealthily did Paris bend his bow,
And on the string he laid a shaft of woe,
And drew it to the point, and aim'd it well.
Singing it sped, and through a shield did go,
And from his barque Protesilaus fell.

XLVIII.

Half gladdened by the omen, through the plain
Went Paris to the walls and mighty gate,
And little heeded he that arrowy rain
The Argive bowmen shower'd in helpless hate.
Nay; not yet feather'd was the shaft of Fate,
His bane, the gift of mighty Heracles
To Philoctetes, lying desolate,
Within a far off island of the seas.

Part 5
THE WAR

The war round Troy, and how many brave men fell, and chiefly
Sarpedon, Patroclus, Hector, Memnon, and Achilles. The coming of
the Amazon, and the wounding of Paris, and his death, and
concerning the good end that Œnone made.

I.

For ten long years the Argive leaguer lay
Round Priam's folk, and wrought them many woes,
While, as a lion crouch'd above his prey,
The Trojans yet made head against their foes;
And as the swift sea-water ebbs and flows
Between the Straits of Hellé and the main,
Even so the tide of battle sank and rose,
And fill'd with waifs of war the Ilian plain.

II.

And horse on horse was driven, as wave on wave;
Like rain upon the deep the arrows fell,
And like the wind, the war-cry of the brave
Rang out above the battle's ebb and swell,
And long the tale of slain, and sad to tell;
Yet seem'd the end scarce nearer than of yore
When nine years pass'd and still the citadel
Frown'd on the Argive huts beside the shore.

III.

And still the watchers on the city's crown
Afar from sacred Ilios might spy
The flame from many a fallen subject town

Flare on the starry verges of the sky,
And still from rich Maeonia came the cry
Of cities sack'd where'er Achilles led.
Yet none the more men deem'd the end was nigh
While knightly Hector fought unvanquished.

IV.

But ever as each dawn bore grief afar,
And further back, wax'd Paris glad and gay,
And on the fringes of the cloud of war
His arrows, like the lightning, still would play;
Yet fled he Menelaus on a day,
And there had died, but Aphrodite's power
Him in a golden cloud did safe convey
Within the walls of Helen's fragrant bower.

V.

But she, in longing for her lord and home,
And scorn of her wild lover, did withdraw
From all men's eyes: but in the night would roam
Till drowsy watchmen of the city saw
A shadowy shape that chill'd the night with awe,
Treading the battlements; and like a ghost,
She stretch'd her lovely arms without a flaw,
In shame and longing, to the Argive host.

VI.

But all day long within her bower she wept,
Still dreaming of the dames renown'd of old,
Whom hate or love of the Immortals swept

Within the toils of Atê manifold;
And most she loved the ancient tales that told
How the great Gods, at length to pity stirr'd,
Changed Niobe upon the mountains cold,
To a cold stone; and Procne to a bird,

VII.

And Myrrha to an incense-breathing tree;—
"And ah," she murmur'd, "that the Gods were kind,
And bade the Harpies lay their hands on me,
And bear me with the currents of the wind
To the dim end of all things, and the blind
Land where the Ocean turneth in his bed:
Then should I leave mine evil days behind,
And Sleep should fold his wings above my head."

VIII.

And once she heard a Trojan woman bless
The fair-haired Menelaus, her good lord,
As brave among brave men, not merciless,
Not swift to slay the captives of his sword,
Nor wont was he to win the gold abhorr'd
Of them that sell their captives over sea,
And Helen sighed, and bless'd her for that word,
"Yet will he ne'er be merciful to me!"

IX.

In no wise found she comfort; to abide
In Ilios was to dwell with shame and fear,
And if unto the Argive host she hied,

Then should she die by him that was most dear.
And still the days dragg'd on with bitter cheer,
Till even the great Gods had little joy,
So fast their children fell beneath the spear,
Below the windy battlements of Troy.

X.

Yet many a prince of south lands, or of east,
For dark Cassandra's love came trooping in,
And Priam made them merry at the feast,
And all night long they dream'd of wars to win,
And with the morning hurl'd into the din,
And cried their lady's name for battle-cry,
And won no more than this: for Paris' sin,
By Diomede's or Aias' hand to die.

XI.

But for one hour within the night of woes
The hope of Troy burn'd steadfast as a star;
When strife among the Argive lords arose,
And dread Achilles held him from the war;
Yea, and Apollo from his golden car
And silver bow his shafts of evil sped,
And all the plain was darken'd, near and far,
With smoke above the pyres of heroes dead.

XII.

And many a time through vapour of that smoke
The shafts of Troy fell fast; and on the plain
All night the Trojan watch fires burn'd and broke

Like evil stars athwart a mist of rain.
And through the arms and blood, and through the slain,
Like wolves among the fragments of the fight,
Crept spies to slay whoe'er forgat his pain
One hour, and fell on slumber in the night.

XIII.

And once, when wounded chiefs their tents did keep,
And only Aias might his weapons wield,
Came Hector with his host, and smiting deep,
Brake bow and spear, brake axe and glaive and shield,
Bulwark and battlement must rend and yield,
And by the ships he smote the foe and cast
Fire on the ships; and o'er the stricken field,
The Trojans saw that flame arise at last!

XIV.

But when Achilles saw the soaring flame,
And knew the ships in peril, suddenly
A change upon his wrathful spirit came,
Nor will'd he that the Danaans should die:
But call'd his Myrmidons, and with a cry
They follow'd where, like foam on a sea-wave
Patroclus' crest was dancing, white and high,
Above the tide that back the Trojans drave.

XV.

But like a rock amid the shifting sands,
And changing springs, and tumult of the deep,
Sarpedon stood, till 'neath Patroclus' hands,

Smitten he fell; then Death and gentle Sleep
Bare him from forth the battle to the steep
Where shines his castle o'er the Lycian dell;
There hath he burial due, while all folk weep
Around the kindly Prince that loved them well.

XVI.

Not unavenged he fell, nor all alone
To Hades did his soul indignant fly,
For soon was keen Patroclus overthrown
By Hector, and the God of archery;
And Hector stripp'd his shining panoply,
Bright arms Achilles lent: ah! naked then,
Forgetful wholly of his chivalry,
Patroclus lay, nor heard the strife of men.

XVII.

Then Hector from the war a little space
Withdrew, and clad him in Achilles' gear,
And braced the gleaming helmet on his face,
And donn'd the corslet, and that mighty spear
He grasped—the lance that makes the boldest fear;
And home his comrades bare his arms of gold,
Those Priam once had worn, his father dear,
But in his father's arms he waxed not old!

XVIII.

Then round Patroclus' body, like a tide
That storms the swollen outlet of a stream
When the winds blow, and the rains fall, and wide

The river runs, and white the breakers gleam,—
Trojans and Argives battled till the beam
Of Helios was sinking to the wave,
And now they near'd the ships: yet few could deem
That arms of Argos might the body save.

XIX.

But even then the tidings sore were borne
To great Achilles, of Patroclus dead,
And all his goodly raiment hath he torn,
And cast the dust upon his golden head,
And many a tear and bitter did he shed.
Ay; there by his own sword had he been slain,
But swift his Goddess-mother, Thetis, sped
Forth with her lovely sea-nymphs from the main.

XX.

For, as a mother when her young child calls
Hearkens to that, and hath no other care:
So Thetis, from her green and windless halls
Rose, at the first word of Achilles' prayer,
To comfort him, and promise gifts of fair
New armour wrought by an immortal hand;
Then like a silver cloud she scaled the air,
Where bright the dwellings of Olympus stand.

XXI.

But, as a beacon from a 'leaguer'd town
Within a sea-girt isle, leaps suddenly,
A cloud by day; but when the sun goes down,

The tongues of fire flash out, and soar on high,
To summon warlike men that dwell thereby
And bid them bring a rescue over-seas,—
So now Athene sent a flame to fly
From brow and temples of Aeacides.

XXII.

Then all unarm'd he sped, and through the throng,
He pass'd to the dyke's edge, beyond the wall,
Nor leap'd the ranks of fighting men among,
But shouted clearer than the clarion's call
When foes on a beleaguer'd city fall.
Three times he cried, and terror fell on these
That heard him; and the Trojans, one and all,
Fled from that shouting of Aeacides.

XXIII.

Backward the Trojans reel'd in headlong flight,
Chariots and men, and left their bravest slain;
And the sun fell; but Troy through all the night
Watch'd by her fires upon the Ilian plain,
For Hector did the sacred walls disdain
Of Ilios; nor knew that he should stand
Ere night return'd, and burial crave in vain,
Unarm'd, forsaken, at Achilles' hand.

XXIV.

But all that night within his chamber high
Hephaestus made his iron anvils ring;
And, ere the dawn, had wrought a panoply,

The goodliest ever worn by mortal king.
This to the Argive camp did Thetis bring,
And when her child had proved it, like the star
That heralds day, he went forth summoning
The host Achaean to delight of war.

XXV.

And as a mountain torrent leaves its bed,
And seaward sweeps the toils of men in spate,
Or as a forest-fire, that overhead
Burns in the boughs, a thing insatiate,
So raged the fierce Achilles in his hate;
And Xanthus, angry for his Trojans slain,
Brake forth, while fire and wind made desolate
What war and wave had spared upon the plain.

XXVI.

Now through the fume and vapour of the smoke
Between the wind's voice and the water's cry,
The battle shouting of the Trojans broke,
And reached the Ilian walls confusedly,
But over soon the folk that watch'd might spy
Thin broken bands that fled, avoiding death,
Yet many a man beneath the spear must die,
Ere by the sacred gateway they drew breath.

XXVII.

And as when fire doth on a forest fall
And hot winds bear it raging in its flight,
And beechen boughs, and pines are ruin'd all,

So raged Achilles' anger in that fight;
And many an empty car, with none to smite
The madden'd horses, o'er the bridge of war
Was wildly whirled, and many a maid's delight
That day to the red wolves was dearer far.

* * * * *

XXVIII.

Some Muse that loved not Troy hath done thee wrong,
Homer! who whisper'd thee that Hector fled
Thrice round the sacred walls he kept so long;
Nay, when he saw his people vanquishèd
Alone he stood for Troy; alone he sped
One moment, to the struggle of the spear,
And, by the Gods deserted, fell and bled,
A warrior stainless of reproach and fear.

XXIX.

Then all the people from the battlement
Beheld what dreadful things Achilles wrought,
For on the body his revenge he spent,
The anger of the high Gods heeding nought,
To whom was Hector dearest, while he fought,
Of all the Trojan men that were their joy,
But now no more their favour might be bought
By savour of his hecatombs in Troy.

XXX.

So for twelve days cheered the Argive host,

Also, presently Patroclus hath to Hades won,

However, Hector bare lay, and still his phantom

Should moan where waters of Cocytus run;

Till Priam did what no man conceived hath done,

Who set out to pass among the Argive groups,

Furthermore, clasp'd the knees of him that large number his
child,

Also, kiss'd his horrendous destructive hands.

XXXI.

At such a cost was Hector's body sent

To Ilios, where the ladies wail'd him deafening;

What's more, Helen's distress brake into mourn

As blasts a lake the hindrances of a slope,

For lost, lost, lost was that one companion who still

Remained by her with kind discourse and delicate heart,

The sword of war, unadulterated confidence, and undaunted
will,

That endeavored to keep all underhanded things separated.

* * *

XXXII.

Thus men covered Hector. Yet, they came,

The Amazons, from frozen fields a far distance.

A counterpart for saints in the loathsome game

Of lances, the dears of the God of War,

Whose coming was to Priam dearer far

Than light to him that is an extended period of time dazzle,

At the point when bloodsucker's hand hath taën away the bar

That vex'd him, or the recuperating God is thoughtful;

XXXIII.

Furthermore, Troy was happy, and with the morning light

The Amazons went forward to kill and kill;

Furthermore, wondrously they drave the enemy in flight,

Until the Sun had wander'd a large portion of his way;

Yet, when he stoop'd to nightfall and the dark

Hour when men free the cow underneath the burden,

No more Achilles held him from the fight,

However, repulsive through the ladies' positions he broke.

XXXIV.

Then, at that point comes overshadow upon the bow safeguard,

What's more, passing on them that bear it, and they fall

One here, one there, about the stricken field,

As in that craftsmanship, of Love remembrance,

Which decays on the heavenly Carian divider.

Ay, still we see, actually love, actually feel sorry for there

The champion house cleaners, so valiant, so god-like tall,

In Time's in spite of enduringly reasonable.

XXXV.

However, as a pigeon that conquers a bird of prey, stood

Penthesilea, fury outcasting dread,

Or on the other hand as a rear, that in the darkling wood

Withstands a lion for her younglings dear;

So stood the young lady before Achilles' lance;

To no end, for singing from his hand it sped,

Also, crash'd through safeguard and breastplate till the sheer

Cold bronze drank blood, and down the sovereign fell dead.

XXXVI.

Then, at that point from her locks the rudder Achilles tore

Also, flaunted o'er the killed; however lo, the face

Of her in this manner lying in the residue and butchery

Seem'd lovelier than is the lady elegance

Of Artemis, when fatigued from the pursuit,

She sleepeth in a spooky dell obscure.

And every one of the Argives marvell'd for a space,

Yet, most Achilles made a weighty groan:

XXXVII.

Furthermore, in his heart there came the exhausted idea

Of all that was, and everything that may have been,

Of all the distress that his sword had fashioned,

Of Death that currently gravitated toward him: of the green

Vales of Larissa, where, with such a sovereign,

With such an adoration as presently his lance had killed,

He had been glad, who should wind the skein

Of offensive conflicts, and ne'er be happy once more.

XXXVIII.

Yea, presently wax'd Fate half exhausted of her game,

Furthermore, had no consideration except for affirmative to kill
and kill,

Also, numerous youthful rulers to the fight came,

Also, of that euphoria they immediately had their fill,

What's more, last came Memnon: and the Trojans still

Cheered up, as wearied sailors that see

(Long toss'd on obscure waves at the breezes' will)

Through mists the sparkling peak of Helikê.

XXXIX.

For Memnon was the offspring of the brilliant Dawn,

A Goddess married to a human lord,

Who harps for ever on the shores removed

That line on the place where there is sun-rising;

What's more, he was sustained near the hallowed spring

That is the secret wellspring, everything being equal,

By them that in the Gods' own nursery sing,

The lily-ladies call'd Hesperides.

XL.

Be that as it may, him the offspring of Thetis in the battle

Met on a blustery winter day, when high

The residue was spun, and wrapp'd them like the evening

That falleth on the mountains subtly

At the point when the floods come, and down their courses dry

The deluges thunder, and lightning flasheth far:

So rang, so sparkled their saddle appallingly

Underneath the blinding thunder-haze of war.

XLI.

Then, at that point the Dawn shudder'd on her brilliant seat,

Also, called unto the West Wind, and he blew

Also, brake the cloud in two; and alone

Achilles stood, yet Memnon, stricken through,

Lay lovely in the midst of the shocking dew

Of fight, and a deathless heart was fain

Of tears, to Gods inconceivable, that drew

From mortal hearts a tad bit of their aggravation.

XLII.

In any case, presently, their chief killed, the Trojans escaped,

What's more, wild Achilles drove them in his disdain,

Avenging still his dear Patroclus dead,

Nor knew the hour with his own destruction was extraordinary,

Nor shuddered, remaining in the Scaean entryway,

Where antiquated prescience predicted his fall;

Then, at that point out of nowhere there sped the electrical jolt,

What's more, destroyed Achilles by the Ilian divider:

XLIII.

From Paris' bow it sped, and even there,

Indeed, even as he grasp'd the skirts of triumph,

Achilles fell, nor any man may dare

From forward the Trojan entryway to draw near;

Be that as it may, as the woodmen watch a lion bite the dust,

Pierced with the tracker's bolt, nor draw close

Till Death hath veil'd his eyelids totally,

All things being equal the Trojans held unapproachable in dread.

XLIV.

Yet, there his colleagues on his wondrous safeguard

Laid the reasonable collection of Achilles killed,

Also, unfortunately uncovered him through the stomped on field,

Also, lo! the deathless ladies of the primary

Ascended, with Thetis, from the blustery plain,

Also, round the dead man excellent they cried,

Bemoaning, and with despairing strain

The sweet-voiced Muses forlornly answered.

XLV.

Yea, Muses and Sea-ladies sang his lament,

Also, powerfully the serenade emerged and harsh,

Also, wondrous echoes answer'd from the flood

Of the dim ocean, and from the blessed slope

Of Ida; and the substantial mists and chill

Were gathering like grievers, pitiful and slow,

Furthermore, Zeus roared powerfully, and fill

The dells and knolls of Ida profound with snow.

XLVI.

Presently Paris was not satisfied with the notoriety

Furthermore, rich award Troy gave his arrow based weaponry;

However, o'er the wine he flaunted that the game

That very night he deem'd to win, or pass on;

"For scant their watch the whirlwind will resist,"

He said, "and all undream'd of might we go,

What's more, fall upon the Argives where they lie,

Concealed, unheard, in the midst of the quiet snow."

XLVII.

Along these lines, flush'd with wine, and clad in garment white

Over their mail, the young fellows follow'd him,

Their aide a blurring pit fire in the evening,

What's more, the ocean's groaning somewhere far off faint.

What's more, still with eddying snow the air swam,

Also, dimly did they wend they knew not where,

White in that reviled night: a military bleak,

'Wilder'd with wine, and visually impaired with spinning air.

XLVIII.

There was an untouchable in the Argive host,

One Philoctetes; whom Odysseus' wile,

(For, save he help'd, the Leaguer everything was lost,)

Drew from his refuge inside the Lemnian isle.

Yet, him individuals, as an outcast abominable,

Despised, and drave to a solitary cottage a remote place,

For injured sore was he, and numerous some time

His cries would wake the host foredone with war.

XLIX.

Presently Philoctetes was a bowman wight;

However, in his quiver had he little store

Of bolts tipp'd with bronze, and feather'd brilliant;

Nay, his were blue with form, and worried o'er

With numerous a spell Melampus created of yesteryear,

Singing over his errand a tune of plague;

What's more, they were venom'd with the Centaur's butchery,

What's more, tipp'd with bones of men an extended period of
time killed.

L.

This lowlife for very torment may only occasionally rest,

Furthermore, that evening dozed not: in the groaning impact

He deem'd the dead with regards to his hovel crawled,

Also, quietly he rose, and round him cast

His attire foul, and from the entryway he pass'd,

Also, peer'd into the evening, and soothly heard

A whisper'd voice; then, at that point gripp'd his bolts quick

Also, hung his bow, and cried a severe word:

LI.

"Craftsmanship thou a gibbering apparition with war outworn,

Also, thy faint life in Hades not started?

Craftsmanship thou a man that holdst my despondency in disdain,

But then dost live, and view the sun?

In the event that man,— methinks thy wonderful days are finished,

Also, thou shalt squirm in torture more terrible than mine;

In the event that apparition,— new agony in Hades hast thou won,

What's more, there with twofold hardship shalt most likely pine."

LII.

He spake, and drew the string, and sent a shaft
At venture through the midnight and the snow,
A little while he listen'd, then he laugh'd
Within himself, a dreadful laugh and low;

For over well the answer did he know
That midnight gave his message, the sharp cry
And armour rattling on a fallen foe
That now was learning what it is to die.

LIII.

Then Philoctetes crawl'd into his den
And hugg'd himself against the bitter cold,
While round their leader came the Trojan men
And bound his wound, and bare him o'er the wold,
Back to the lights of Ilios; but the gold
Of Dawn was breaking on the mountains white,
Or ere they won within the guarded fold,
Long 'wilder'd in the tempest and the night.

LIV.

And through the gate, and through the silent street,
And houses where men dream'd of war no more,
The bearers wander'd with their weary feet,
And Paris to his high-roof'd house they bore.
But vainly leeches on his wound did pore,
And vain was Argive Helen's magic song,
Ah, vain her healing hands, and all her lore,
To help the life that wrought her endless wrong.

LV.

Slow pass'd the fever'd hours, until the grey
Cold light was paling, and a sullen glow
Of livid yellow crown'd the dying day,
And brooded on the wastes of mournful snow.

Then Paris whisper'd faintly, "I must go
And face that wild wood-maiden of the hill;
For none but she can win from overthrow
Troy's life, and mine that guards it, if she will."

LVI.

So through the dumb white meadows, deep with snow,
They bore him on a pallet shrouded white,
And sore they dreaded lest an ambush'd foe
Should hear him moan, or mark the moving light
That waved before their footsteps in the night;
And much they joy'd when Ida's knees were won,
And 'neath the pines upon an upland height,
They watch'd the star that heraldeth the sun.

LVII.

For under woven branches of the pine,
The soft dry needles like a carpet spread,
And high above the arching boughs did shine
In frosty fret of silver, that the red
New dawn fired into gold-work overhead:
Within that vale where Paris oft had been
With fair Œnone, ere the hills he fled
To be the sinful lover of a Queen.

LVIII.

Not here they found Œnone: "Nay, not here,"
Said Paris, faint and low, "shall she be found;
Nay, bear me up the mountain, where the drear
Winds walk for ever on a haunted ground.

Methinks I hear her sighing in their sound;
Or some God calls me there, a dying man.
Perchance my latest journeying is bound
Back where the sorrow of my life began."

LIX.

They reach'd the gateway of that highest glen
And halted, wond'ring what the end should be;
But Paris whisper'd Helen, while his men
Fell back: "Here judged I Gods, here shalt thou see
What judgment mine old love will pass on me.
But hide thee here; thou soon the end shalt know,
Whether the Gods at length will set thee free
From that old net they wove so long ago."

LX.

Ah, there with wide snows round her like a pall,
Œnone crouch'd in sable robes; as still
As Winter brooding o'er the Summer's fall,
Or Niobe upon her haunted hill,
A woman changed to stone by grief, where chill
The rain-drops fall like tears, and the wind sighs:
And Paris deem'd he saw a deadly will
Unmoved in wild Œnone's frozen eyes.

LXI.

"Nay, prayer to her were vain as prayer to Fate,"
He murmur'd, almost glad that it was so,
Like some sick man that need no longer wait,
But his pain lulls as Death draws near his woe.

And Paris beckon'd to his men, and slow
They bore him dying from that fatal place,
And did not turn again, and did not know
The soft repentance on Œnone's face.

LXII.

But Paris spake to Helen: "Long ago,
Dear, we were glad, who never more shall be
Together, where the west winds fainter blow
Round that Elysian island of the sea,
Where Zeus from evil days shall set thee free.
Nay, kiss me once, it is a weary while,
Ten weary years since thou hast smiled on me,
But, Helen, say good-bye, with thine old smile!"

LXIII.

And as the dying sunset through the rain
Will flush with rosy glow a mountain height,
Even so, at his last smile, a blush again
Pass'd over Helen's face, so changed and white;
And through her tears she smiled, his last delight,
The last of pleasant life he knew, for grey
The veil of darkness gather'd, and the night
Closed o'er his head, and Paris pass'd away.

LXIV.

Then for one hour in Helen's heart re-born,
Awoke the fatal love that was of old,
Ere she knew all, and the cold cheeks outworn,
She kiss'd, she kiss'd the hair of wasted gold,

The hands that ne'er her body should enfold;
Then slow she follow'd where the bearers led,
Follow'd dead Paris through the frozen wold
Back to the town where all men wish'd her dead.

LXV.

Perchance it was a sin, I know not, this!
Howe'er it be, she had a woman's heart,
And not without a tear, without a kiss,
Without some strange new birth of the old smart,
From her old love of the brief days could part
For ever; though the dead meet, ne'er shall they
Meet, and be glad by Aphrodite's art,
Whose souls have wander'd each its several way.

* * * * *

LXVI.

And now was come the day when on a pyre
Men laid fair Paris, in a broider'd pall,
And fragrant spices cast into the fire,
And round the flame slew many an Argive thrall.
When, like a ghost, there came among them all,
A woman, once beheld by them of yore,
When first through storm and driving rain the tall
Black ships of Argos dash'd upon the shore.

LXVII.

Not now in wrath Œnone came; but fair
Like a young bride when nigh her bliss she knows,
And in the soft night of her fallen hair
Shone flowers like stars, more white than Ida's snows,
And scarce men dared to look on her, of those
The pyre that guarded; suddenly she came,
And sprang upon the pyre, and shrill arose
Her song of death, like incense through the flame.

LXVIII.

And still the song, and still the flame went up,
But when the flame wax'd fierce, the singing died;
And soon with red wine from a golden cup
Priests drench'd the pyre; but no man might divide
The ashes of the Bridegroom from the Bride.
Nay, they were wedded, and at rest again,
As in those old days on the mountain-side,
Before the promise of their youth was vain.

Part 6
THE SACK OF TROY. THE RETURN OF HELEN

The sack of Troy, and of how Menelaus would have let stone Helen, but Aphrodite saved her, and made them at one again, and how they came home to Lacedaemon, and of their translation to Elysium.

I.

There came a day, when Trojan covert operatives viewed

How, o'er the Argive leaguer, all the air

Was unadulterated of smoke, no fight racket there swell'd,

Nor any clarion-call was sounding there!

Yea, of the serried boats the strand was uncovered,

Also, ocean and shore were still, as quite a while in the past

At the point when Ilios knew not Helen, and the reasonable

Sweet face that makes eternal all her misfortune.

II.

So for a space the watchers on the divider

Were quiet, wond'ring what these things may mean.

In any case, at the last, sent couriers to call

Priam, and every one of the seniors, and the lean

Remainder of goodly bosses, that whenever had been

The safeguard and stay of Ilios, and her bliss,

Nor yet despair'd, however confided in Gods inconspicuous,

Also, cast their lances, and shed their blood for Troy.

III.

They came, the more part dim, become early old,

In war and plague; yet with them was the youthful

Coroebus, that yet late had left the overlay

Also, herds of sheep Maeonian slopes among,

Furthermore, boldly his parcel with Priam flung,

For adoration for an act of futility and a reasonable face,—

The eyes that once the God of Pytho sung,

That presently look'd obscurely to the butcher spot.

IV.

Presently while the seniors kept their long discussion,

Coroebus took unnoticed to his band,

What's more, driven a small bunch by a postern door

Across the plain, across the infertile land

Where when the glad plants were wont to stand,

What's more, 'mid the groups once did ladies sing,—

In any case, presently the plain was squander on each hand,

However to a great extent a bloom would inhale of Spring.

V.

So quick across the stomped on war zone

Unchallenged still, however attentive, did they pass,

By numerous a wrecked lance or shatter'd safeguard

That in Fate's hour selected shifty was:

Just the heron cried from the bog

Close by, and ravens, and the dim

Wolves left their devouring in the tangled grass,

Hesitant; and loiter'd, nor escaped far away.

VI.

There lurk'd no lances in the high stream banks,

No snare by the cairns of men outworn,

Yet, void stood the hovels, in terrible positions,

Where men through this load of numerous years had borne

Wild summer, and the gnawing winter's disdain;

What's more, here a blade was left, and there a bow,

Be that as it may, ruinous seem'd all things and desolate,

As in some camp neglected quite a while in the past.

VII.

Glutted wolves crawled round the raised areas, and ate

The tissue of casualties that the clerics had killed,

Also, wild canines battled over the hallowed meat

Late offer'd to the deathless Gods to no end,

By men that, for remuneration of all their aggravation,

Should pull the ropes, and fatigued at the paddle,

Or on the other hand, suffocating, grasp at froth in the midst of the principle,

Nor win their asylum on the Argive shore.

VIII.

Not long the young fellows marvell'd at the sight,

Yet, getting a handle on one a sword, and one the lance

Aias, or Tydeus' child, had borne in battle,

They sped, and fill'd the town with happy cheer,

For society were fast the glad information to hear,

Furthermore, pour'd through every one of the doors into the plain,

Cheering as they wander'd all over,

O'er the long Argive works suffered to no end.

IX.

Ok, sweet it was, without the city dividers,

To hear the birds coo, and the finches sing;

Ok, sweet, to twine their actual loves coronals

Of woven breeze blossoms, and each fragrant thing

That blooms in the strides of the spring;

Also, sweet, to lie, neglectful of their sorrow,

Where violets trail by waters meandering,

Also, the wild fig-tree putteth forward his leaf!

X.

Presently while they wander'd as they would, they found

Something wondrous: a wonder of man's ability,

That remained inside a vale of empty ground,

What's more, bulk'd scant more modest than the severe slope,—

The normal hand truck that the dead men fill

Who passed on in the long leaguer,— not of earth,

Was this new omen, yet of tree, and still

The Trojans stood, and marvell'd 'mid their jollity.

XI.

Ay, much they wonder'd what this thing may be,

Molded like a Horse it was; and numerous a stain

There show'd upon the strong light emissions,

For some with fire were blacken'd, some with downpour

Were wet and dim in the midst of white boards of plane,

New cut among the trees that presently were not many

On squandered Ida; yet men looked to no end,

Nor truth thereof as far as their looking might be aware.

XII.

Finally they deem'd it was something holy,

Vow'd to Poseidon, ruler of the profound,

Furthermore, that herewith the Argives pray'd the King

Of wind and wave to hush the oceans to rest;

So this, they cried, inside the holy keep

Of Troy should rest, dedication of the conflict;

Furthermore, sturdily they haled it up the precarious,

Furthermore, dragg'd the beast to their dividers far off.

XIII.

The entire day they fashioned: and kids crown'd with blossoms

Laid light hands on the ropes; elderly people men would employ

Their weak power; so through the joyful hours

They toil'd, middle chuckling and sweet minstrelsy,

What's more, late they attracted the incomparable Horse to the high

Peak of the slope, and wide the tall doors swang;

In any case, threefold, for all their power, it stood accordingly

Unaffected, and threefold like stricken protective layer rang.

XIV.

Natheless they created their will; then, at that point raised area fires

The Trojans constructed, and did the Gods beg

To give satisfaction of every happy longing.

However, from the cups the wine they probably won't pour,

The tissue upon the spits did squirm and thunder,

The smoke developed red as blood, and numerous an appendage

Of casualties leap'd upon the sanctuary floor,

Shaking; and moans in the midst of the churches faint

XV.

Rang low, and from the reasonable Gods' pictures

What's more, from their eyes, dropp'd sweat and numerous a
tear;

The dividers with blood were dribbling, and on these

That forfeited, came frightfulness and incredible dread;

The heavenly shrubs to Apollo dear

Adjacent to his sanctuary blurred abruptly,

What's more, wild wolves from the mountains drew anear,

What's more, ravens through the sanctuaries seem'd to fly.

XVI.

However still the men of Troy were happy on a fundamental level,

Furthermore, o'er peculiar meat they revell'd, similar to people fey,

However each would shiver on the off chance that he looked separated,

For round their knees the fogs were gather'd dark,

Like covers on men that Hell-ward take their direction;

However, joyfully withal they ate consequently,

Also, laugh'd with warped lips, and oft would say

Some insidious sounding word and inauspicious.

XVII.

Also, Hecuba among her youngsters spake,

"Allow each man to pick the meat he liketh best,

For bread not any more together will we break.

Nay, soon from all my work must I rest,

Be that as it may, eat ye well, and drink the red wine, in case

Ye fault my home wifery among men dead."

And all they took her expression for a joke,

Also, pleasantly did they giggle at that she said.

XVIII.

Then, at that point, similar to a raven on the of night,

The wild Cassandra bounced all over,

As yet crying, "Accumulate, assemble for the battle,

Also, support the cap on, and handle the lance,

For lo, the armies of the Night are here!"

So shriek'd the terrifying prophetess divine.

However, all men mock'd, and were of joyful cheer;

Protected as the Gods they deem'd them, o'er their wine.

XIX.

Until further notice with minstrelsy the air was sweet,

The delicate spring air, and thick with incense smoke;

Also, groups of cheerful artists down the road

Flew from the blossom crown'd entryways, and wheel'd, and broke;

Also, cherishing words the adolescents and ladies talked,

For Aphrodite did their hearts bewilder,

As when underneath dim sinkhole or green oak

The shepherd men and ladies meet and grin.

XX.

No guard they set, for truly to them all
Did Love and slumber seem exceeding good;
There was no watch by open gate nor wall,
No sentinel by Pallas' image stood;
But silence grew, as in an autumn wood
When tempests die, and the vex'd boughs have ease,
And wind and sunlight fade, and soft the mood
Of sacred twilight falls upon the trees.

XXI.

Then the stars cross'd the zenith, and there came
On Troy that hour when slumber is most deep,
But any man that watch'd had seen a flame
Spring from the tall crest of the Trojan keep;
While from the belly of the Horse did leap
Men arm'd, and to the gates went stealthily,
While up the rocky way to Ilios creep
The Argives, new return'd across the sea.

XXII.

Now when the silence broke, and in that hour
When first the dawn of war was blazing red,
There came a light in Helen's fragrant bower,
As on that evil night before she fled
From Lacedaemon and her marriage bed;
And Helen in great fear lay still and cold,
For Aphrodite stood above her head,
And spake in that sweet voice she knew of old:

XXIII.

"Beloved one that dost not love me, wake!
Helen, the night is over, the dawn is near,
And safely shalt thou fare with me, and take
Thy way through fire and blood, and have no fear:
A little hour, and ended is the drear
Tale of thy sorrow and thy wandering.
Nay, long hast thou to live in happy cheer,
By fair Eurotas, with thy lord, the King."

XXIV.

Then Helen rose, and in a cloud of gold,
Unseen amid the vapour of the fire,
Did Aphrodite veil her, fold on fold;
And through the darkness, thronged with faces dire,
And o'er men's bodies fallen in a mire
Of new spilt blood and wine, the twain did go
Where Lust and Hate were mingled in desire,
And dreams and death were blended in one woe.

XXV.

Fire and the foe were masters now: the sky
Flared like the dawn of that last day of all,
When men for pity to the sea shall cry,
And vainly on the mountain tops shall call
To fall and end the horror in their fall;
And through the vapour dreadful things saw they,
The maidens leaping from the city wall,
The sleeping children murder'd where they lay.

XXVI.

Yea, cries like those that make the hills of Hell
Ring and re-echo, sounded through the night,
The screams of burning horses, and the yell
Of young men leaping naked into fight,
And shrill the women shriek'd, as in their flight
Shriek the wild cranes, when overhead they spy
Between the dusky cloud-land and the bright
Blue air, an eagle stooping from the sky.

XXVII.

And now the red glare of the burning shone
On deeds so dire the pure Gods might not bear,
Save Ares only, long to look thereon,
But with a cloud they darken'd all the air.
And, even then, within the temple fair
Of chaste Athene, did Cassandra cower,
And cried aloud an unavailing prayer;
For Aias was the master in that hour.

XXVIII.

Man's lust won what a God's love might not win,
And heroes trembled, and the temple floor
Shook, when one cry went up into the din,
And shamed the night to silence; then the roar
Of war and fire wax'd great as heretofore,
Till each roof fell, and every palace gate
Was shatter'd, and the King's blood shed; nor more
Remain'd to do, for Troy was desolate.

XXIX.

Then dawn drew near, and changed to clouds of rose
The dreadful smoke that clung to Ida's head;
But Ilios was ashes, and the foes
Had left the embers and the plunder'd dead;
And down the steep they drove the prey, and sped
Back to the swift ships, with a captive train,—
While Menelaus, slow, with drooping head,
Follow'd, like one lamenting, through the plain.

XXX.

Where death might seem the surest, by the gate
Of Priam, where the spears raged, and the tall
Towers on the foe were falling, sought he fate
To look on Helen once, and then to fall,
Nor see with living eyes the end of all,
What time the host their vengeance should fulfil,
And cast her from the cliff below the wall,
Or burn her body on the windy hill.

XXXI.

But Helen found he never, where the flame
Sprang to the roofs, and Helen ne'er he found
Where flock'd the wretched women in their shame
The helpless altars of the Gods around,
Nor lurk'd she in deep chambers underground,
Where the priests trembled o'er their hidden gold,
Nor where the armed feet of foes resound
In shrines to silence consecrate of old.

XXXII.

So wounded to his hut and wearily
Came Menelaus; and he bow'd his head
Beneath the lintel neither fair nor high;
And, lo! Queen Helen lay upon his bed,
Flush'd like a child in sleep, and rosy-red,
And at his footstep did she wake and smile,
And spake: "My lord, how hath thy hunting sped,
Methinks that I have slept a weary while!"

XXXIII.

For Aphrodite made the past unknown
To Helen, as of old, when in the dew
Of that fair dawn the net was round her thrown:
Nay, now no memory of Troy brake through
The mist that veil'd from her sweet eyes and blue
The dreadful days and deeds all over-past,
And gladly did she greet her lord anew,
And gladly would her arms have round him cast.

XXXIV.

Then leap'd she up in terror, for he stood
Before her, like a lion of the wild,
His rusted armour all bestain'd with blood,
His mighty hands with blood of men defiled,
And strange was all she saw: the spears, the piled
Raw skins of slaughter'd beasts with many a stain;
And low he spake, and bitterly he smiled,
"The hunt is ended, and the spoil is ta'en."

XXXV.

No more he spake; for certainly he deem'd
That Aphrodite brought her to that place,
And that of her loved archer Helen dream'd,
Of Paris; at that thought the mood of grace
Died in him, and he hated her fair face,
And bound her hard, not slacking for her tears;
Then silently departed for a space,
To seek the ruthless counsel of his peers.

XXXVI.

Now all the Kings were feasting in much joy,
Seated or couch'd upon the carpets fair
That late had strown the palace floors of Troy,
And lovely Trojan ladies served them there,
And meat from off the spits young princes bare;
But Menelaus burst among them all,
Strange, 'mid their revelry, and did not spare,
But bade the Kings a sudden council call.

XXXVII.

To mar their feast the Kings had little will,
Yet did they as he bade, in grudging wise,
And heralds call'd the host unto the hill
Heap'd of sharp stones, where ancient Ilus lies.
And forth the people flock'd, as throng'd as flies
That buzz about the milking-pails in spring,
When life awakens under April skies,
And birds from dawning into twilight sing.

XXXVIII.

Then Helen through the camp was driven and thrust,
Till even the Trojan women cried in glee,
"Ah, where is she in whom thou put'st thy trust,
The Queen of love and laughter, where is she?
Behold the last gift that she giveth thee,
Thou of the many loves! to die alone,
And round thy flesh for robes of price to be
The cold close-clinging raiment of sharp stone."

XXXIX.

Ah, slowly through that trodden field and bare
They pass'd, where scarce the daffodil might spring,
For war had wasted all, but in the air
High overhead the mounting lark did sing;
Then all the army gather'd in a ring
Round Helen, round their torment, trapp'd at last,
And many took up mighty stones to fling
From shards and flints on Ilus' barrow cast.

XL.

Then Menelaus to the people spoke,
And swift his wing'd words came as whirling snow,
"Oh ye that overlong have borne the yoke,
Behold the very fountain of your woe!
For her ye left your dear homes long ago,
On Argive valley or Boeotian plain;
But now the black ships rot from stern to prow,
Who knows if ye shall see your own again?

XLI.

"Ay, and if home ye win, ye yet may find,
Ye that the winds waft, and the waters bear
To Argos! ye are quite gone out of mind;
Your fathers, dear and old, dishonour'd there;
Your children deem you dead, and will not share
Their lands with you; on mainland or on isle,
Strange men are wooing now the women fair,
And love doth lightly woman's heart beguile.

XLII.

"These sorrows hath this woman wrought alone:
So fall upon her straightway that she die,
And clothe her beauty in a cloak of stone!"
He spake, and truly deem'd to hear her cry
And see the sharp flints straight and deadly fly;
But each man stood and mused on Helen's face,
And her undream'd-of beauty, brought so nigh
On that bleak plain, within that ruin'd place.

LXIII.

And as in far off days that were to be,
The sense of their own sin did men constrain,
That they must leave the sinful woman free
Who, by their law, had verily been slain,
So Helen's beauty made their anger vain,
And one by one his gather'd flints let fall;
And like men shamed they stole across the plain,
Back to the swift ships and their festival.

XLIV.

But Menelaus look'd on her and said,
"Hath no man then condemn'd thee,—is there none
To shed thy blood for all that thou hast shed,
To wreak on thee the wrongs that thou hast done.
Nay, as mine own soul liveth, there is one
That will not set thy barren beauty free,
But slay thee to Poseidon and the Sun
Before a ship Achaian takes the sea!"

XLV.

Therewith he drew his sharp sword from his thigh
As one intent to slay her: but behold,
A sudden marvel shone across the sky!
A cloud of rosy fire, a flood of gold,
And Aphrodite came from forth the fold
Of wondrous mist, and sudden at her feet
Lotus and crocus on the trampled wold
Brake, and the slender hyacinth was sweet.

XLVI.

Then fell the point that never bloodless fell
When spear bit harness in the battle din,
For Aphrodite spake, and like a spell
Wrought her sweet voice persuasive, till within
His heart there lived no memory of sin,
No thirst for vengeance more, but all grew plain,
And wrath was molten in desire to win
The golden heart of Helen once again.

XLVII.

Then Aphrodite vanish'd as the day
Passes, and leaves the darkling earth behind;
And overhead the April sky was grey,
But Helen's arms about her lord were twined,
And his round her as clingingly and kind,
As when sweet vines and ivy in the spring
Join their glad leaves, nor tempests may unbind
The woven boughs, so lovingly they cling.

* * * * *

XLVIII.

Noon long was over-past, but sacred night
Beheld them not upon the Ilian shore;
Nay, for about the waning of the light
Their swift ships wander'd on the waters hoar,
Nor stay'd they the Olympians to adore,
So eagerly they left that cursed land,
But many a toil, and tempests great and sore,
Befell them ere they won the Argive strand.

XLIX.

To Cyprus and Phoenicia wandering
They came, and many a ship, and many a man
They lost, and perish'd many a precious thing
While bare before the stormy North they ran,
And further far than when their quest began
From Argos did they seem,—a weary while,—
Becalm'd in sultry seas Egyptian,
A long day's voyage from the mouths of Nile.

L.

But there the Gods had pity on them, and there
The ancient Proteus taught them how to flee
From that so distant deep,—the fowls of air
Scarce in one year can measure out that sea;
Yet first within Aegyptus must they be,
And hecatombs must offer,—quickly then
The Gods abated of their jealousy,
Wherewith they scourge the negligence of men.

LI.

And strong and fair the south wind blew, and fleet
Their voyaging, so merrily they fled
To win that haven where the waters sweet
Of clear Eurotas with the brine are wed,
And swift their chariots and their horses sped
To pleasant Lacedaemon, lying low
Grey in the shade of sunset, but the head
Of tall Taygetus like fire did glow.

LII.

And what but this is sweet: at last to win
The fields of home, that change not while we change;
To hear the birds their ancient song begin;
To wander by the well-loved streams that range
Where not one pool, one moss-clad stone is strange,
Nor seem we older than long years ago,
Though now beneath the grey roof of the grange
The children dwell of them we used to know?

LIII.

Came there no trouble in the later days
To mar the life of Helen, when the old
Crowns and dominions perish'd, and the blaze
Lit by returning Heraclidae roll'd
Through every vale and every happy fold
Of all the Argive land? Nay, peacefully
Did Menelaus and the Queen behold
The counted years of mortal life go by.

LIV.

"Death ends all tales," but this he endeth not;
They grew not grey within the valley fair
Of hollow Lacedaemon, but were brought
To Rhadamanthus of the golden hair,
Beyond the wide world's end; ah never there
Comes storm nor snow; all grief is left behind,
And men immortal, in enchanted air,
Breathe the cool current of the Western wind.

LV.

But Helen was a Saint in Heathendom,
A kinder Aphrodite; without fear
Maidens and lovers to her shrine would come
In fair Therapnae, by the waters clear
Of swift Eurotas; gently did she hear
All prayers of love, and not unheeded came
The broken supplication, and the tear
Of man or maiden overweigh'd with shame.

O'er Helen's shrine the grass is growing green,
In desolate Therapnae; none the less
Her sweet face now unworshipp'd and unseen
Abides the symbol of all loveliness,
Of Beauty ever stainless in the stress
Of warring lusts and fears;—and still divine,
Still ready with immortal peace to bless
Them that with pure hearts worship at her shrine.

Note

[In this story in rhyme of the fortunes of Helen, the theory that she was an unwilling victim of the Gods has been preferred. Many of the descriptions of manners are versified from the Iliad and the Odyssey. The description of the events after the death of Hector, and the account of the sack of Troy, is chiefly borrowed from Quintus Smyrnaeus.]

The person and history of Helen of Troy have been considered in altogether different manners by writers and mythologists. In endeavoring to follow the central current of old customs about Helen, we can't actually get further back than the Homeric sonnets, the Iliad and Odyssey. Philological guess might guarantee us that Helen, as the majority of the characters of old sentiment, is "just the Dawn," or Light, or some other splendid being moved by Paris, who addresses Night, or Winter, or the Cloud, or another force of obscurity. Without examining these thoughts, it very well might be said that the Greek writers (at all occasions before figurative clarifications of folklore came in, around 500 years before Christ) viewed Helen basically as a lady of magnificent magnificence. Homer was not thinking about the Dawn, or the Cloud when he portrayed Helen among the Elders on the Ilian dividers, or rehashed her regret over the dead group of Hector. The Homeric sonnets are our most established scholarly records about Helen, however it is plausible enough that the artist has changed and cleaned more old customs which actually get by in different pieces of Greek legend. In Homer Helen is consistently the girl of Zeus. Isocrates advises us ("Helena," 211 b) that "while large numbers of the mythical beings were offspring of Zeus, he thought the paternity of none of his little girls worth guaranteeing, save that of Helen just." In Homer, then, at that point, Helen is the little girl of Zeus, however Homer avoids mentioning the renowned legend which causes Zeus to expect the type of a swan to charm the mother of Helen. Unhomeric as this legend is, we might view it as very old. Very much like stories of pursuit and transformation, for amorous or different purposes, among the old legends of Wales, and in the "Bedouin Nights," just as

184

in the fantasies of Australians and Red Indians. Once more, the conviction that various groups of humankind dive from creatures, as from the Swan, or from divine beings looking like creatures, is found in each quarter of the world, and among the rudest races. Numerous Australian locals of to-day guarantee plummet, similar to the regal place of Sparta, from the Swan. The Greek fantasies wavered with respect to whether Nemesis or Leda was the lady of the hour of the Swan. Homer just notices Leda among "the spouses and little girls of powerful men," whose apparitions Odysseus viewed in Hades: "And I saw Leda, the renowned associate of Tyndareus, who uncovered to Tyndareus two children, solid of heart, Castor, tamer of horses, and the fighter Polydeuces." These saints Helen, in the Iliad (iii. 238), portrays as her mom's children. In this way, if Homer has any particular view regarding the matter, he holds that Leda is the mother of Helen by Zeus, of the Dioscuri by Tyndareus.

Greek thoughts concerning the personality of Helen fluctuated with the different dispositions of Greek writing. Homer's own thoughts regarding his courageous woman are presumably best communicated in the words with which Priam welcomes her as she shows up among the gathered older folks, who are watching the Argive legends from the mass of Troy:— "In nowise, dear youngster, do I fault you; nay, the Gods are at fault, who have stirred against me the woful conflict of the Achaeans." Homer, similar to Priam, tosses the blame of Helen on the Gods, however it isn't extremely straightforward precisely what he implies by saying "the Gods are to be faulted." in any case, Homer evades the mental issues wherein present day verse revels, by crediting practically all progressions of the temperaments of men to divine motivation. In this way when Achilles, in a renowned entry of the main book of the Iliad, sets up his half-attracted blade the sheath, and doesn't kill Agamemnon, Homer relegates his atonement to the immediate impact of Athene. Once more, he says in the Odyssey, about Clytemnestra, that "she would none of the foul deed;" that is of the adoration for Aegisthus, till "the destruction of the Gods bound her to her ruin." So far a similar pardon is made for the dangerous Clytemnestra with respect to the obliging Helen. Once more, Homer is, in the strictest sense, and in solid difference to the Greek playwrights and to Virgil, a gallant writer. It would presumably be difficult to track down a section in which he talks brutally or severely of the lead of any reasonable and honorable woman. The shameful unfairness of Eriphyle, who sold her ruler for gold, wins for her the appellation "contemptuous;" and Achilles, in a snapshot of solid pain, applies a term of severe dislike to Helen. Yet, Homer is too gallant to even consider passing judgment on the existence of any woman, and just shows the opposite side of the courageous person—its remorselessness to people not of honorable birth—in depicting the "foul demise" of the holding up ladies of Penelope. "God deny that I should take these ladies' lives by a spotless demise," says Telemachus (Odyssey, xxii. 462). So "pretty much the entirety of their necks nooses were projected that they may bite the dust by the passing generally melancholy. Also, they squirmed with their feet for a little space, yet for no extended period of time." In attempting to comprehend Homer's gauge of Helen, in this way, we should consider his hypothesis of help from above, and for his courageous judgment of women. However, there are two entries in the Iliad which might be taken as showing Homer's perspective that Helen was in a real sense a casualty, a reluctant casualty, of Aphrodite, and that she was moved forcibly a hostage from Lacedaemon. These sections are in the Iliad, ii. 356, 590. In the previous text Nestor says, "let none be anxious to get back ere he has framed with a Trojan's better half, and retaliated for the longings and distresses of Helen"— τίσσθαι δέλένης ορμηματα τε στοναχας τε. It is along these lines that Mr. Gladstone, a prominent hero of Helen's, would deliver this section, and a similar understanding was supported by the old "Separatists" (Chorizontes), who wished to demonstrate that the Iliad and Odyssey were by various creators; however numerous specialists like to interpret "to vindicate our works and distresses for the wellbeing of Helen"— "to retaliate for all that we have suffered in the endeavor to win back Helen." Thus the proof of this entry is vague. The more pleasant approach to look for Homer's genuine perspective on Helen is to analyze every one of the sections where she happens. The outcome will be something like this:— Homer finds in Helen a being of the most extraordinary individual appeal and beauty of character; a lady who attributes to herself coerce a lot more noteworthy than the genuine proportion of her offense. She is at any point delicate besides with the Goddess who deceived her, and the contemptible sweetheart whose parcel she is constrained to share. Against them her defenseless resentment breaks out in glimmers of articulate disdain. Homer was obviously familiar with the legend of Helen's catch by Theseus, a fantasy delineated in the enhancements of the coffer of Cypselus. In any case, we first see Helen, the reason for the conflict, when Menelaus and Paris are going to battle their duel for the good of she, in the 10th year of the Leaguer (Iliad, iii. 121). Iris is shipped off gather Helen to the dividers. She discovers Helen in her chamber, weaving at a powerful loom, and weaving on embroidered artwork the undertakings of the attack—the skirmishes of pony subduing Trojans and bronze-clad Achaeans. The message of Iris reestablishes in Helen's heart "a sweet longing for her master and her own city, and them that conceived her;" in this way, hung in shiny white, Helen goes with her three ladies to the dividers. There, over the entryway, similar to some lord in the Old Testament, Paris sits among his advocates, and they are totally astounded at Helen's magnificence; "no wonder is it that Trojans and Achaeans languish long and tired works over such a lady, so wondrous prefer to the godlike goddesses." Then Priam, guaranteeing Helen that he holds her irreproachable, offers her name to him her kinsfolk and the other Achaean heroes. In her answer, Helen shows that beauty of contrition which is positively not regularly found in antiquated writing:— "Would that detestable passing had been my decision, when I followed thy child, and left my marriage arbor and my family, and my little girl dear, and the ladies of like age with me." Agamemnon she calls, "the spouse's sibling of me improper; oh well, that a particularly one ought to be." She names a significant number of the champions, yet misses her siblings Castor and Polydeuces, "own siblings of mine, one mother uncovered us. Possibly they followed not from lovely Lacedaemon, or here they continued in quick ships, yet presently they have no heart to go down into the fight for fear of the disgrace and many censures that are mine."

"So spake she, however currently the nurturing earth covered them, there in Lacedaemon, in their own dear country."Menelaus and Paris fought out their duel, the Trojan was discomfited, but was rescued from death and carried to Helen's bower by Aphrodite. Then the Goddess came in disguise to seek Helen on the wall, and force her back into the arms of her defeated lover. Helen turned on the Goddess with an abruptness and a force of sarcasm and invective which seem quite foreign to her gentle nature. "Wilt thou take me further yet to some city of Phrygia or pleasant Maeonia, if there any man is dear to thee … Nay, go thyself and sit down by Paris, and forswear the paths of the Gods, but ever lament for him and cherish him, till he make thee his wife, yea, or perchance his slave, but to him will I never go." But this anger of Helen is soon overcome by fear, when the Goddess, in turn, waxes wrathful, and Helen is literally driven by threats—"for the daughter of Zeus was afraid,"— into the arms of Paris. Yet even so she taunts her lover with his cowardice, a cowardice which she never really condones. In the sixth book of the Iliad she has been urging him to return to the war. She then expresses her penitence to Hector, "would that the fury of the wind had borne me afar to the mountains, or the wave of the roaring sea—ere ever these ill deeds were done!" In this passage too, she prophesies that her fortunes will be αοίδιμοι εσσομένοισι famous in the songs, good or evil, of men unborn. In the last book of the Iliad we meet Helen once more, as she laments over the dead body of Hector. "'Never, in all the twenty years since I came hither, have I heard from thee one taunt or one evil word: nay, but if any other rebuked me in the halls, any one of my husband's brothers, or of their sisters, or their wives, or the mother of my husband (but the king was ever gentle to me as a father), then wouldst thou restrain them with thy loving kindness and thy gentle speech.' So spake she; weeping."

In the Odyssey, Helen is once more in Lacedaemon, the honoured but still penitent wife of Menelaus. How they became reconciled (an extremely difficult point in the story), there is nothing in Homer to tell us.

Sir John Lubbock has conjectured that in the morals of the heroic age Helen was not really regarded as guilty. She was lawfully married, by "capture," to Paris. Unfortunately for this theory there is abundant proof that, in the heroic age, wives were nominally*bought* for so many cattle, or given as a reward for great services. There is no sign of marriage by capture, and, again, marriage by capture is a savage institution which applies to unmarried women, not to women already wedded, as Helen was to Menelaus. Perhaps the oldest evidence we have for opinion about the later relations of Helen and Menelaus, is derived from Pausanias's (174. a.d.) description of the Chest of Cypselus. This ancient coffer, a work of the seventh century, b.c., was still preserved at Olympia, in the time of Pausanias. On one of the bands of cedar or of ivory, was represented (Pausanias, v. 18), "Menelaus with a sword in his hand, rushing on to kill Helen—clearly at the sacking of Ilios." How Menelaus passed from a desire to kill Helen to his absolute complacency in the Odyssey, Homer does not tell us. According to a statement attributed to Stesichorus (635, 554, b.c.?), the army of the Achaeans purposed to stone Helen, but was overawed and compelled to relent by her extraordinary beauty: "when they beheld her, they cast down their stones on the ground." It may be conjectured that the reconciliation followed this futile attempt at punishing a daughter of Zeus. Homer, then, leaves us without information about the adventures of Helen, between the sack of Tiny and the reconciliation with Menelaus. He hints that she was married to Deiphobus, after the death of Paris, and alludes to the tradition that she mimicked the voices of the wives of the heroes, and so nearly tempted them to leave their ambush in the wooden horse. But in the fourth book of the Odyssey, when Telemachus visits Lacedaemon, he finds Helen the honoured wife of Menelaus, rich in the marvellous gifts bestowed on her, in her wanderings from Troy, by the princes of Egypt.

"While yet he pondered these things in his mind and in his heart, Helen came forth from her fragrant vaulted chamber, like Artemis of the golden arrows; and with her came Adraste and set for her the well-wrought chair, and Alcippe bare a rug of soft wool, and Phylo bare a silver basket which Alcandre gave her, the wife of Polybus, who dwelt in Thebes of Egypt, where is the chiefest store of wealth in the houses. He gave two silver baths to Menelaus, and tripods twain, and ten talents of gold. And besides all this, his wife bestowed on Helen lovely gifts; a golden distaff did she give, and a silver basket with wheels beneath, and the rims thereof were finished with gold. This it was that the handmaid Phylo bare and set beside her, filled with dressed yarn, and across it was laid a distaff charged with wool of violet blue. So Helen sat her down in the chair, and beneath was a footstool for the feet."

When the host and guests begin to weep the ready tears of the heroic age over the sorrows of the past, and dread of the dim future, Helen comforts them with a magical potion.

"Then Helen, daughter of Zeus, turned to new thoughts. Presently she cast a drug into the wine whereof they drank, a drug to lull all pain and anger, and bring forgetfulness of every sorrow. Whoso should drink a draught thereof, when it is mingled in the bowl, on that day he would let no tear fall down his cheeks, not though his mother and his father died, not though men slew his brother or dear son with the sword before his face, and his own eyes beheld it. Medicines of such virtue and so helpful had the daughter of Zeus, which Polydamna, the wife of Thon, had given her, a woman of Egypt, where Earth the grain-giver yields herbs in greatest plenty, many that are healing in the cup, and many baneful."

So Telemachus was kindly entertained by Helen and Menelaus, and when he left them it was not without a gift.

"And Helen stood by the coffers wherein were her robes of curious needlework which she herself had wrought. Then Helen, the fair lady, lifted one and brought it out, the widest and most beautifully embroidered of all, and it shone like a star, and lay far beneath the rest."

190

Presently, we read, "Helen of the fair face came up with the robe in her hands, and spake: 'Lo! I too give thee this gift, dear child, a memorial of the hands of Helen, for thy bride to wear upon the day of thy desire, even of thy marriage. But meanwhile let it lie with thy mother in her chamber. And may joy go with thee to thy well-builded house, and thine own country.'"

Helen's last words, in Homer, are words of good omen, her prophecy to Telemachus that Odysseus shall return home after long wanderings, and take vengeance on the rovers. We see Helen no more, but Homer does not leave us in doubt as to her later fortunes. He quotes the prophecy which Proteus, the ancient one of the sea, delivered to Menelaus:—

"But thou, Menelaus, son of Zeus, art not ordained to die and meet thy fate in Argos, the pasture-land of horses, but the deathless gods will convey thee to the Elysian plain and the world's end, where is Rhadamanthus of the fair hair, where life is easiest for men. No snow is there, nor yet great storm, nor any rain; but alway ocean sendeth forth the breeze of the shrill West to blow cool on men: yea, for thou hast Helen to wife, and thereby they deem thee to be son of Zeus."

We must believe, with Isocrates, that Helen was translated, with her lord, to that field of Elysium, "where falls not hail, or rain, or any snow." This version of the end of Helen's history we have adopted, but many other legends were known in Greece. Pausanias tells us that, in a battle between the Crotoniats and the Locrians, one Leonymus charged the empty space in the Locrian line, which was entrusted to the care of the ghost of Aias. Leonymus was wounded by the invisible spear of the hero, and could not be healed of the hurt. The Delphian oracle bade him seek the Isle of Leuke in the Euxine Sea, where Aias would appear to him, and heal him. When Leonymus returned from Leuke he told how Achilles dwelt there with his ancient comrades, and how he was now wedded to Helen of Troy. Yet the local tradition of Lacedaemon showed the sepulchre of Helen in Therapnae. According to a Rhodian legend (adopted by the author of the "Epic of Hades"), Helen was banished from Sparta by

191

the sons of Menelaus, came wandering to Rhodes, and was there strangled by the servants of the queen Polyxo, who thus avenged the death of her husband at Troy. It is certain, as we learn both from Herodotus (vi. 61) and from Isocrates, that Helen was worshipped in Therapnae. In the days of Ariston the king, a deformed child was daily brought by her nurse to the shrine of Helen. And it is said that, as the nurse was leaving the shrine, a woman appeared unto her, and asked what she bore in her arms, who said, "she bore a child." Then the woman said, "show it to me," which the nurse refused, for the parents of the child had forbidden that she should be seen of any. But the woman straitly commanding that the child should be shown, and the other beholding her eagerness, at length the nurse showed the child, and the woman caressed its face and said, "she shall be the fairest woman in Sparta." And from that day the fashion of its countenance was changed, "and the child became the fairest of all the Spartan women."

It is a characteristic of Greek literature that, with the rise of democracy, the old epic conception of the ancient heroes altered. We can scarcely recognize the Odysseus of Homer in the Odysseus of Sophocles. The kings are regarded by the tragedians with some of the distrust and hatred which the unconstitutional tyrants of Athens had aroused. Just as the later *chansons de geste* of France, the poems written in an age of feudal opposition to central authority, degraded heroes like Charles, so rhetorical, republican, and sophistical Greece put its quibbles into the lips of Agamemnon and Helen, and slandered the stainless and fearless Patroclus and Achilles.

The Helen of Euripides, in the "Troades," is a pettifogging sophist, who pleads her cause to Menelaus with rhetorical artifice. In the "Helena," again, Euripides quite deserts the Homeric traditions, and adopts the late myths which denied that Helen ever went to Troy. She remained in Egypt, and Achaeans and Trojans fought for a mere shadow, formed by the Gods out of clouds and wind. In the "Cyclops" of Euripides, a satirical drama, the cynical giant is allowed to speak of Helen in a strain of coarse banter. Perhaps the essay of Isocrates on Helen may be regarded as a kind of answer to the attacks of several speakers in the works of the tragedians. Isocrates defends Helen simply on the plea of her beauty: "To Heracles Zeus gave strength, to Helen beauty, which naturally rules over even strength itself." Beauty, he declares, the Gods themselves consider the noblest thing in the world, as the Goddesses showed when they contended for the prize of loveliness. And so marvellous, says Isocrates, was the beauty of Helen, that for her glory Zeus did not spare his beloved son, Sarpedon; and Thetis saw Achilles die, and the Dawn bewailed her Memnon. "Beauty has raised more mortals to immortality than all the other virtues together." And that Helen is now a Goddess, Isocrates proves by the fact that the sacrifices offered to her in Therapnae, are such as are given, not to heroes, but to immortal Gods.

When Rome took up the legends of Greece, she did so in no chivalrous spirit. Few poets are less chivalrous than Virgil; no hero has less of chivalry than his pious and tearful Aeneas. In the second book of the Aeneid, the pious one finds Helen hiding in the shrine of Vesta, and determines to slay "the common curse of Troy and of her own country." There is no glory, he admits, in murdering a woman:—

Extinxisse nefas tamen et sumpsisse merentis
Laudabor poenas, animumqne explesse juvabit
Ultricis flammae, et cineres satiasse meorum.

But Venus appears and rescues the unworthy lover of Dido from the crowning infamy which he contemplates. Hundreds of years later, Helen found a worthier poet in Quintus Smyrnaeus, who in a late age sang the swan-song of Greek epic minstrelsy. It is thus that (in the fourth century a.d.) Quintus describes Helen, as she is led with the captive women of Ilios, to the ships of the Achaeans:—"Now Helen lamented not, but shame dwelt in her dark eyes, and reddened her lovely cheeks, … while around her the people marvelled as they beheld the flawless grace and winsome beauty of the woman, and none dared upbraid her with secret taunt or open rebuke. Nay, as she had been a Goddess they beheld her gladly, for dear and desired was she in their sight. And as when their own country appeareth to men

193

long wandering on the sea, and they, being escaped from death and the deep, gladly put forth their hands to greet their own native place; even so all the Danaans were glad at the sight of her, and had no more memory of all their woful toil, and the din of war: such a spirit did Cytherea put into their hearts, out of favour to fair Helen and father Zeus." Thus Quintus makes amends for the trivial verses in which Coluthus describes the flight of a frivolous Helen with an effeminate Paris.

To follow the fortunes of Helen through the middle ages would demand much space and considerable research. The poets who read Dares Phrygius believed, with the scholar of Dr. Faustus, that "Helen of Greece was the admirablest lady that ever lived." When English poetry first found the secret of perfect music, her sweetest numbers were offered by Marlowe at the shrine of Helen. The speech of Faustus is almost too hackneyed to be quoted, and altogether too beautiful to be omitted:—

Was this the face that launched a thousand ships,
And burnt the topless towers of Ilium!
Sweet Helen, make me immortal with a kiss.
Her lips suck forth my soul! see where it flies;
Come, Helen, come, give me my soul again;
Here will I dwell, for heaven is in those lips,
And all is dross that is not Helena.

* * * * *

Oh thou art fairer than the evening air
Clad in the beauty of a thousand stars.

The loves of Faustus and Helen are readily allegorized into the passion of the Renaissance for classical beauty, the passion to which all that is not beauty seemed very dross. This is the idea of the second part of "Faust," in which Helen once more became, as she prophesied in the Iliad, a song in the mouths of later men. Almost her latest apparition in English poetry, is in the "Hellenics" of Landor. The sweetness of the character of Helen; the tragedy of the

194

death of Corythus by the hand of his father Paris; and the omnipotence of beauty and charm which triumph over the wrath of Menelaus, are the subjects of Landor's verse. But Helen, as a woman, has hardly found a nobler praise, in three thousand years, than Helen, as a child, has received from Mr. Swinburne in "Atalanta in Calydon." Meleager is the speaker:—

Even such (for sailing hither I saw far hence,
And where Eurotas hollows his moist rock
Nigh Sparta, with a strenuous-hearted stream)
Even such I saw their sisters; one swan-white,
The little Helen, and less fair than she
Fair Clytemnestra, grave as pasturing fawns
Who feed and fear some arrow; but at whiles,
As one smitten with love or wrung with joy,
She laughs and lightens with her eyes, and then
Weeps; whereat Helen, having laughed, weeps too,
And the other chides her, and she being chid speaks naught,
But cheeks and lips and eyelids kisses her
Laughing, so fare they, as in their bloomless bud
And full of unblown life, the blood of gods.

There is all the irony of Fate in Althaeas' reply

Sweet days befall them and good loves and lords,
Tender and temperate honours of the hearths,
Peace, and a perfect life and blameless bed.

Printed in Poland
by Amazon Fulfillment
Poland Sp. z o.o., Wrocław
23 February 2024

1ad20de3-b4b8-4712-a73a-a77aa61db0e9R01